"An inspiring true story."
- Author Woodrow Polston

MIRACLES ON
THE CANCER
JOURNEY

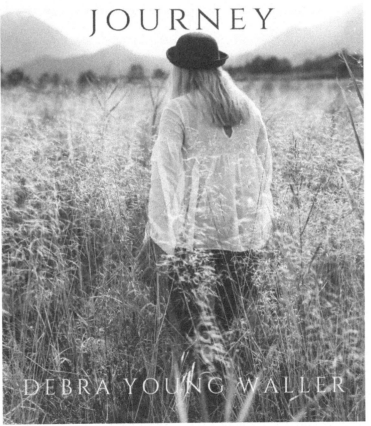

DEBRA YOUNG WALLER

Debra Young Waller

MIRACLES ON THE CANCER JOURNEY

POLSTON HOUSE
PUBLISHING

DEBRA YOUNG WALLER

Debra Young Waller

MIRACLES ON THE CANCER JOURNEY

Published by Polston House Publishing LLC
www.Polstonhouse.com

Published in the United States of America

Acknowledgements

Thank you, Judy, time after time you helped me get Larry back and forth from the hospital and cancer center when I wasn't able to. You soothed our souls with your inspiring words of hope. You brought us comfort during a hard journey. When Larry was passing to the other side, you and your daughter, Katie, helped each one of us deal with such a tough time. We are, and always will be family.

My Dad, spoke with unwavering words of faith. He has always been my rock of stability as he quoted the words of faith through the scriptures. My Brother, Al, followed with those words of faith quoted from the Bible as well.

My Mom, had, in the past, gone through the cancer journey and Shared her testimony of how God healed her. She is cancer free today.

Charlotte, thank you for taking us to lunch and all your words of encouragement. Patiently, you listened to all of our medical questions. Thank you for being available with your extensive detailed medical knowledge.

Wesley Waller, thank you for showing up at the right times to bring laughter to our hearts; laughter does the heart good like a medicine. You also ministered to our family by being a handyman. Larry knew he could count on you to help us with things around the house that needed fixing.

To our church family and Pastor, Reverend Carl McKalip, thank you for being a prayer warrior. You, Sandy (my cousin) and (her husband) Kenny always reached out and have been the best examples of God's love.

You, Sandy, have held my hand in prayer as well as you and Kenny paying us visits to encourage us. Even though there were times when Larry was needing someone to understand his battle of independence, but so dependent upon our help. The frustrations he had at times needed an understanding heart, which you both gave to him freely and graciously.

Pastor Jack and Paula Morgan thank you for giving us love and support. Thank you for allowing us to preach hope to those who didn't understand our stance on faith while going through this cancer journey.

On Christmas day, 2016, when we found out our Grandson, Ezekiel died in the womb, while I was at the hospital with Jake and Josie, our grown kids, you both showed up to be with Larry who had collapsed at the news of Ezekiel who had died Christmas morning. You both stayed with Larry at our house while he laid in bed exhausted from the grief of the loss of his grandson.

Miracles on the Cancer Journey

My dear friend Carrie thank you for orchestrating and bringing together the fundraising singings to help, not only with the medical expenses but uplifting our spirits with the sweet songs sung. God used you and the awesome Gospel groups to raise funds to help us get through all of these medical expenses we faced on this cancer journey.

In acknowledgment, the Association of International Assemblies, where I work. In specific, you helped me to apply for Larry's Social Security Disability so that we would be able to get our income in order.

Thank you to all of our loved ones who not only brought love and support during the trial but continuing to encourage my family and I as we encounter the feeling of grief in our lives and courageously go forward on our journey called life.

As an extension of my late husband, Larry and I, God has blessed us with the beautiful support group of family. As I name each one, I feel a deep gratitude to the service of love each had displayed to me as well as their dad, father-in-law and future father-in-law.

I will start with my oldest son, Jacob Young. You stood in the gap as my helper, working on my car when it needed to be fixed. You showed amazing emotional strength along with your beautiful wife, Josie. Josie Young, thank you for all the meals you made us, and though you are soft spoken your strong faith values encouraged us tremendously.

In acknowledgment to James Young, my youngest, and his then fiancé, Heather Scoggin, now Heather Young, I give tribute. James, you always made us laugh and tried to keep our hearts light. You two teamed up with the amazing grace that can only come from God. You guys endured day and night, staying by Larry's side those four long months and caring for him. The hospice nurse and CNA were especially touched as they witnessed such love and compassion that was shown. When others in the past got tired and gave up the fight, you Heather, spent long hours typing and editing this book while James encouraged you. James knew this was God's way of leaving a legacy for his Dad so others may grow in grace and be encouraged to follow Christ.

These four, along with our granddaughter, Cheyla, were my 'Dream Team'. Every time Larry would look at his beautiful granddaughter, Cheyla, he would light up. As I look back, I see how God walked with not only Larry on this cancer journey, but also our friends and family through, as well as myself. I realize so many miracles that cannot be measured by size, but by impact. Only God could have done this!

"But grow [spiritually mature] in the grace and knowledge of our Lord and Savior Jesus Christ. To Him be the glory (honor, majesty, splendor), both now and to the day of eternity. Amen." (2 Peter 3:18 Amp)

PREFACE

This day God has blessed me with an ice storm that has forced our office to close, and it puts me in a place where I can think long and hard on these past four years. I guess, today is the perfect day for journalism. Today, I choose new beginning.

There needed to be a place to vent. Writing a journal releases the compounded feelings of disappointment, and ongoing frustrations that I deal with every time this roller coaster dips into a downward slide of events. It's hard to express to others what I feel, because I know I've always been my family's encourager throughout the years whenever they get down.

I know the Lord, in His word, tells us that He is in control. Somehow, though, I battle with the conflict between the evidence that I see and the scripture that reads;

"And we know [with great confidence] *that God* [who is deeply concerned about us] *causes all things to work together* [as a plan] *for good for those who love God, to those who are called according to His plan and purpose."* (Romans 8:28 Amp)

This life has been quite a journey. When I think back about how much I have been through in these past four years, it seems overwhelming. Although I never dreamed my life would take me through so much change, I learned how to rely solely on the Lord and His strength. I have seen many peaks and valleys, but in hindsight, all have shown God's love and grace. Regardless of life's circumstances His love and mercy are always there.

I know everybody goes through life's hardships at some point. But we don't always stop and think, 'This is what the fire feels like'. 'I know that my attitude will determine how I go through this fire. This can either make or break me, so I choose to trust the Lord with all my heart.'

To be honest with you, I don't feel like trusting the Lord. My emotions tell me otherwise. But my love for God pushes past those disappointed moments when I want to ask why? When I remember the past, I can reflect on the times that God has carried me through to a place in my heart where I said, 'So that is what God was doing'.

Each person's journey is different, but should end up at the destination of Heaven where we will spend eternity.

Brennan Manning, American Author, and public speaker explains the journey this way, "Suffering, failure, loneliness, sorrow, discouragement and death will be part of your journey. The Kingdom of God will conquer all these horrors. No evil can resist grace!"

Miracles on the Cancer Journey

My journey in this book describes how God intertwined His thoughts into my heart while I was trying to figure it all out in my analytical mind. When we don't understand, we have to come up with a conclusion to satisfy our soul which is our emotions.

Isaiah 55:8 shares what is in the heart of God. "For my thoughts are not your thoughts, neither are your ways my ways, saith the Lord." Then the Lord goes on further saying in verse 9, "For as the heavens are higher than your ways, and my thoughts than your thoughts."

God leads the blind in the way they know not. It is like putting a blindfold over a person's eyes and taking them by the hand. We have to trust that the Great I AM will lead us to a safe place on our journey.

As I watched how my grown children responded to the almost four years of their Dad suffering through the cancer treatments, the faith and experiences of trusting the Lord while they were growing up had prepared them for this part of their journey as well as my own.

They, as well as myself, had seen how the Lord answered prayers while we were waiting upon Him to fulfill his promises through His word, which is His will.

We taught our sons the Word of God since they were toddlers. The greatest gift we gave them was to know Christ and Him crucified. Larry would have Bible quizzes with the boys not knowing that one day as they had hid the word and the promises of God through His word in their hearts, would produce faith at the time they needed it the most.

There are many stumbling blocks in the path of our journey. When we stub a toe from rocks in our path, it definitely hurts. There is pain, but in time there is healing from the injury.

I remember the scripture that tells us that God gives us beauty for ashes. Isaiah 61:3. "To bestow on them a crown of beauty instead of ashes, the oil of joy instead of mourning, and a garment of praise instead of a spirit of despair. They will be called oaks of righteousness, a planting of the Lord for the display of his splendor."

When our heart becomes broken from seeing our loved ones go through something, we want to rescue them and do all that we can to bring them comfort through their pain. The Bible says for us to "Bear ye one another's burdens, and so fulfill the law of Christ." Galatians 6:2.

There are those times when we pray, when we have nothing else to offer to the loved one who is suffering. But only to be by their side holding their hand. Job's friends made the mistake of thinking there was something the afflicted loved one did to deserve this type of suffering. How wrong they were. My youngest son said, "Mom, sometimes stuff happens."

Job suffered as a just man who was going through a test of faith. He experienced one of the greatest examples of 'going through the fire'. At the end, God gave Job double recompense for his affliction. Job's journey was accompanied by the glory of God as the Lord watched over him not allowing him to be overwhelmed with grief. Job, before the fire of life took place, had a close relationship with God.

Sometimes we don't realize when God's amazing grace is present in our lives on our journey of affliction. "Weeping may endure for a night but joy comes in the morning." Psalm 30:5.

My Sons, Jacob and James Young, had experienced watching their Dad pass away but not without the glory of God being present while they comforted one another. They knew where their Dad went and they knew life as it was, would be changed forever.

We choose to think on the good things, on the things of good report. I read a quote which said, "There may be a thousand good things that happen in a day, but when that one thing happens which is devastating or disappointing, our minds refocus on the one bad thing and forget about the thousand good things which should have outweighed and lightened the thought of that one negative event."

I have a choice and you have a choice. This is where I roll my works upon the Lord. Then "He will cause my thoughts to become agreeable with His will. Then my plans will be established and then I will have good success." Proverbs 16:3-7.

Success is never giving up, failure is quitting before God has a chance to work on our behalf. As an example and a child of God, giving up is not an option. For without faith it's impossible to please God. But with this statement, in Hebrews 11:6 the Lord brings us into a deeper word of encouragement which says, "For he that cometh to God must believe that He is, and that He is a rewarder of them that diligently seek him."

1

The Beginning of the Cancer Journey

When Larry, my late husband, faced major medical issues in 2013, he decided to make an appointment to be seen by his doctor. When our bodies go through something, we fix it with medicine. Well, that is the normal routine in life, to fix what is broken.

After he was examined, the doctor decided to do a PSA (prostate-specific antigen) test. His test results came back over 200 count. A normal count would have been 0-2. At this moment, we were informed Larry could possibly have cancer. We then, were referred to a specialist.

After a biopsy was done, the doctor set an appointment to explain the over-the-phone diagnose of state 4 Prostate cancer. I was shocked and stunned to hear this news. Our grown Son Jacob, his fiance Josie and our other son, James and our best friend, Judy gathered in the doctor's waiting room. When the doctor shared the diagnosis and what was involved in making this diagnosis, we were all shocked. I looked at Judy and she looked at me with such disappointment and disbelief. How could this be happening to our family!

My husband Larry's first diagnosis after his biopsy held the status: stage four prostate cancer and the doctor's assumption that he had six months or less to live. My faith was challenged. This diagnosis rocked my world.

The sound of silence filled the air. No one spoke, no one had the right words to express, but the look on each one's face said more than words ever could have said. As the doctor broke it down to us what stage 4 meant, we all listened intently not truly realizing what he was meaning. This type of education was about to unfold to take us on a whole new journey that we didn't ask for.

The doctor said this is an aggressive type of cancer spread in the bone and lymph nodes. Without treatment, Larry would have maybe six months to live. The specialist introduced us to what is called, 'hormone therapy'. If the hormone therapy didn't work and his body was to reject it, there would be nothing else they could do.

We all looked at Larry, husband, father and friend. All of a sudden, he spoke up with a smile on his face. The man of God inspired by the glory of God who shined the light in the midst of the darkness, like a lighthouse giving light to the ships at sea.

Larry with great faith and enthusiasm exclaimed, "Doctor, I know what you said is the diagnosis, but I have a God who gave me a promise that by the stripes of Jesus Christ I am healed. I choose to believe God's word!" Larry continued proclaiming his promises of God to the doctor. The doctor looked extremely surprised with a smile that reflected wonder and amazement. The look on the doctor's face said it all. He lit up because, you see, faith is contagious and brings hope to the hearer. The doctor was bewildered and taken off guard.

Judy and I looked at each other again. This time, we both smiled because we just witnessed a miracle of faith empowered by grace. We knew in our hearts that everything would be okay. Each one of us in that room felt the faith arise and felt the presence of the Lord.

I know the doctor on the other hand was, at this time, an unbeliever, full of facts and experience, and past disappointments as his diagnosis took the steering wheel of procedures and treatments. The patients at stage 4 terminal illness would ultimately meet their doom of death. This doctor was what we call an unbeliever. When we all stood to leave, the doctor said, "Good luck". We knew at this point that luck would have nothing to do with it but, the power of God working in each one of us.

'Jesus calls us to be His witnesses.' When some Christians hear this word, they worry that they need exceptional skill or charisma in order to share the good news with others. Yet to witness is not to merely speak of the 'Plan of Salvation' to someone. The word literally means to see, hear, or know by personal presence and perception; to testify; bear witness to; give or afford evidence of. When John wrote that, he was sharing what he had experienced first-hand, he was saying, "I am full of joy because of the experience of knowing Jesus, and I want to invite you to share in that joy!" Dr. Charles Stanley, Pastor and founder of In Touch Ministries said.

After our little meeting in the doctor's room, we all stepped outside the hospital to go home. Larry spoke up with much enthusiasm, "I'm hungry, where do we go to eat!" He had a twinkle in his eyes as he expressed satisfaction to be able to have the last word when death was spoken over him. I remember the word that explains this event well, Proverbs 18:21 "Death and life are in the power of the tongue." Larry chose life, and his actions backed up his words of life.

We have always come through the dark tunnels of life with hope riding piggy back on faith. There were always testimonies shared with the hearer as faith arose in their hearts. God has always made a way when there seemed to be no way. This circumstance in our hearts was no different. We simply believed that with God all things are possible. Now, we come to a new level of faith in God while we put one foot in front of the other. "We walk by faith and not by sight." 2 Corinthians 5:7.

This is how, "the joy of the Lord is our strength". Nehemiah 8:10. The joy of the Lord is found when the human soul feels the squeeze of darkness that surrounds it's very being. We can all tap into the amazing grace giving us the joy that is not determined by human reasoning but, comes from the throne of God. Abraham experienced this type of joy that is rooted in hope. Romans 4:18, "Who against hope believed in hope, that he might become the father of many nations, according to that which was spoken, So shall thy seed be.

Larry experienced that Hope against hope when human reasoning ended. The supernatural hope then, kicked in as he believed God that with God all things are possible to him that believes. This type of hope produces the fruit of Joy that comes from deep within the spirit, but affects the soul.

Debra Young Waller

2

What a Support Team!

After the word spread about Larry being diagnosed with stage four cancer, people from all over our area immediately offered themselves to be a blessing through word or deed. What an amazing support team of loved ones and church family who stepped up to the plate to offer to help in one way or another. We never felt left alone. They now knew that Larry was out of his job working for a local catholic school and church. My small income was all we now had to rely upon when Larry's job had been the main source of income.

Larry was weak and needed to use a walker to keep from falling at this stage of the cancer journey. A close friend of ours gave him a walker while our dear friend, Carrie, brought the church family together to each help us with meals to lighten the burden while we were regrouping with a new strategy in life.

Visitors came to see us to share their testimonies of how God brought them through their trial by fire. My A.I.G.A. (Association of International Gospel Assemblies) office where I worked helped me help Larry file for social security disability. I, otherwise had no idea where to start and Larry definitely wasn't able to handle all the paperwork involved. The process would most likely take at least six months for his disability to kick in.

My Co-workers, Alan Rayl, Cheryl and others did their best to bring support to me while I needed to stay strong for Larry. Alan Rayl always took time to come to the office where Larry volunteered at A.I.G.A. Larry was always glad to see Alan, who at times even brought Larry small gifts to cheer him up. After Larry passed away, I gave those things to my sons. All these people had done their part to be a blessing. This reminds me of where the Bible states in Galatians 6:2 to "bear one another's burdens." Each one did their part to lighten our load. These were those to whom Larry always preached the words of faith, and these are those who are now returning the love back to our family.

A person doesn't realize what a sweet fragrance of love and compassion can surface in the midst of a drought in life. This unexpected devastation of the worst possible scenario sprung up with such an overwhelming feeling that, yes, in this cold dark world there is still a light that continuously overwhelms even the darkest night.

We walk by faith, not by sight as God continues to lead the blind in the way they know not. Each step we took on this cancer journey is like Larry being the broken cracked vessel being used for God's purposes to water the hard ground of the hearts of others for many years. The Lord uses imperfect people. He takes the foolish things to confound the wise. What Satan meant for harm, God will use for our good. Now Larry has become a different type of vessel, a vessel of honor fit for the Master's use. Times like these have a way of bringing out the best in people. The Lord has demonstrated His love through those around us to express who He is. God is love and those who walk in love are his ambassadors. They allow God to work in them to be his hands and feet.

Many have stood in the gap through prayer. Prayer has been and always will be the key to unlock hope and expectation. Thanksgiving and praise follow as we continue to make our requests known to God. In the name of Jesus, we pray the promises, and know that God hears even our faintest cries.

The unseen hope kicks in to become the reality of answered prayer. God sees each sparrow fall. We who are created in the image of God are valued much more than the value of a sparrow. Our hope is that our God can work all things for our good, Romans 8:28, "And we know (with great confidence) that God (who is deeply concerned about us) causes all things to work together (as a plan) for good for those who love God, to those who are called according to His plan and purpose."

Our dear friend, Carrie, got word about our financial situation. Larry wasn't getting his income which would accumulate to six months before the social security disability would kick in. Carrie organized through the Rose of Sharon Full Gospel Temple located at DeSoto, Missouri, a special gospel singing fund raiser event. Several gospel groups donated their time and talent to help raise money for Larry. Our family was extremely grateful for the love shown toward us, which was much needed. These acts of kindness will never be forgotten, how God used them all to send a message to us that we were not alone.

3

Faith With Works; The Power Team

As I reflect back through each chapter of this cancer journey, I know without a doubt, that our faith as a family has been inspired by the Word of God. In the past, we have experienced many miracles in our full-time ministry which we traveled with for over seventeen years. Now, as we walk out our faith in a whole new level, we put one foot in front of the other. It's hard to see what's ahead of us in this dark path, but our simple faith and trust in God. helps us understand that somehow everything will be okay in the end of this journey.

We just know we have to keep on keeping on and choose to obey the Word of God. To think on the good things, the things of good report. Philippians 4:8 gives us the road map to peace in our soul which is our emotions. "Whatever is true, whatever is noble, whatever is right, whatever is pure, whatever is lovely, whatever is admirable, if anything is excellent or praiseworthy, think about such things." We have a God-given imagination to be used for good and not evil. We have been given a gift mingled with grace to be obedient to this simple command which brings peace. If there's *anything* we can do in our trials, it is to think on the good things. Think on the times in the past when God had come through for us. This is a form of faith, with works, which produces the fruits of the spirit.

Larry continued to believe for the best while working at resting Hebrews 4:11,12, "Let us therefore make every effort to enter the rest (of God, to know and experience it for ourselves), so that no one will fall by following the same example of disobedience (as those who died in the wilderness). For the Word of God is living and active and full of power, making it operative, energizing and effective).

My amazing husband knew all those years how to trust the Lord, how God always made a way when there seemed to be no way. He held up the banner of faith as he preached those sermons after his diagnosis with great conviction. God continued to use him greatly even when he sat in a chair in front of the congregations proclaiming the goodness of God. Yes! He continued preaching on divine healing and as we laid hands on others accompanied with the spoken word of faith, and watched as people received their healing.

The episodes we endured during the duration of almost four years of the cancer journey were so complex and contrary to what Larry and I believed about divine healing. It is so conflicting in our natural reasoning when we believe in divine healing and walk the journey of a terminal illness or a chronic condition that lingers on. Some may fall by the wayside in their faith when it is shaken this way when they try to understand and comprehend what faith in God really means.

Miracles on the Cancer Journey

When Larry, the man of God, was faced with this controversial evidence, he continued preaching the divine Word of Truth just as it is quoted in the Bible, "By His stripes we are healed" Isaiah 53:5. He and I both have seen the evidence of healing in others as we laid hands on the sick and they recovered merely by the spoken word. We, even now, still believe in the promises of God.

God is a God who cannot lie. I now realize when we are faced with affliction; sickness and disease, the battle you and I go through are mixed in the circumstance with many elements that are unseen. One, is the will of the individual. When a loved one is dying, and they choose to go home to heaven, we can't go against their will. We can though, pray for them to desire to see their purpose ahead of them. Sometimes when hardship hits a person, there could be bad choices and bad habits they are wrestling with. When a person for instance, breaks the law, they have to pay the consequence for their action. Once in a while, there will be a mercy call where the person repents with a complete turn-a-round and God delivers them from the consequences

One of the ways Larry reached out by faith mingled with his works was, when he started a healing school in our church. Several times a month he held a service specifically speaking on divine healing and broke it down in the scriptures. Those who showed up were few, but hungry to hear the words of faith so that they could share what they've heard to those who were hurting. One particular Sister in Christ was Charlotte. She is a retired nurse who had experienced many cases while working for years in an emergency room. Now, she was able to get an education through the Living Word of God. Hope against hope when doctors give you a bad report, God gives the word of truth inspired by the Holy Ghost.

"The word of God became flesh and dwelt among men." John 1:14. What a mixture of facts with truth that overrides those facts. Thus, creates a miracle to those who believe.

The demonstration Larry displayed during this cancer journey spoke louder than words. He kept the praise on his lips and his testimony through his actions and attitude gave glory to God. His works with his faith became a powerful team. Little do we realize that others are watching us to see how we will react and respond while we are in the fire of life. Because of Larry's love for God and trusted in His promises, He never lost not even one day to self-pity. Can we all follow this example? God said we can. "When we are weak, He is strong." 2 Corinthians 12:9-10. "But he has said to me, My grace is sufficient for you (My loving (kindness and My mercy are more than enough, always available, regardless of the situation); for My power is being perfected (and is completed and shows itself most effectively) in (your) weakness. Therefore, I will all the more gladly boast in my weaknesses, so that the power of Christ (may completely enfold me and) may dwell in me.) So I am well pleased with weaknesses, with insults with distresses, with persecutions, and with difficulties, for the sake of Christ for when I am weak (In human strength), then I am strong (truly able, truly powerful, truly drawing from God's strength).

Debra Young Waller

4

Purpose in the Pain

I truly don't believe God puts sickness on his children. Yes, we are in a decaying world altered by sin. The seeds of sickness, disease and affliction are all around us. We, thus, are in a corrupted world. This planet was created by God, displayed from the taste of God. Heaven will have no corruption, neither sickness nor pain. When sin was brought into the world, it brought its furnishings of death and destruction from the fall of man. When we receive Christ we no longer are under the curse of the law of sin and death. We are new creatures in Christ, the hope of glory.

Unfortunately our bodies are still flesh and are exposed to the elements of this world. There is a devil who came to kill, steal and destroy but, Jesus came to give us life and that more abundantly. John 10:10. Through the blood of Jesus who died for our sins, we sit in heavenly places with Him. Ephesians 2:6. Jesus Christ the Son of God gave us the Keys to the kingdom Matthew 16:19. We therefore, have the power in His name to bind and loosen. So, whatever you bind on earth will have already been bound in heaven, and whatever you loose (permit, declare lawful) on earth will have (already) been loosed in heaven.

When I get thoughts of defeat or despair, immediately the Lord steps up to the plate, He who is the

Prince of Peace, Isaiah 9:1. Thoughts of what if Larry dies, what is in my future when so many years we were a team in ministry, I have learned through the Word to cast down imaginations and every high thing that exalteth itself against the knowledge of God and bringing into captivity every thought to the obedience of Christ. 2 Corinthians 10:5. This is what we call again, work at resting.

The fight of faith is real, but when I meditated on the promises of God and His road map, I too didn't lose any quality of life. For a few minutes or a day, I fought the fight of faith. This is a real struggle to those who see what's going on around them, but learn to focus on what they can't see so what they can't see eventually becomes more real to them. The unseen spiritual world where our invisible God sits on His throne watches intentional to show himself strong, 2 Chronicles 16:9.

When I reflect back in time, I can see purpose in the pain. The road map of God's way of doing things and how He has equipped me and Larry through the living Word of God, which unfolds for those who read this book showing how to walk out their journey victoriously.

We can all say one day, 'I've been there, I know what you are going through and this is how the Lord helped me to walk through the valley of the shadow of death. This is how I was able to hold on to God's hand while walking through the afflictions of life. This is how I was able to not lose my peace and my joy.' "Weeping may endure for a night but joy comes in the morning." Psalm 30:5.

Life needs to have purpose or life is in vain. The one who builds his life upon the sand, when the storms of life hit, they will surely fall. But, those who build their house upon the rock of Jesus Christ, they know their name is written in the Lamb's book of life. God knows how to take what's wrong and make something beautiful come out of it.

We get only one chance to live life and make it count. Walking with the Lord and loving others should be our main purpose. What springs up from within our very being is the fruit that is a direct result of knowing how much God loves us. This creates a pure trust in the Lord that He knows what he is doing in our lives when we face hardship. Knowing we have purpose and a destiny eases the suffering in life. Our testimony is the power behind our sermons when we go through hard times of how the Lord delivered us, so then we can say, 'only God'.

Debra Young Waller

5

Beauty for Ashes

How amazing God is when we see our lives unfold, how He can give beauty for ashes as in Isaiah 61. When a man or woman commits to pray and call upon the name of the Lord, when they pray, the words are mixed with praise and thanksgiving, mountains are moved in ways they have never dreamed of. Our soul is revived when we give the sacrifice of praise. Many times when I chose to believe, I didn't feel like it, but I had to make a choice to trust the Lord with all my heart. God sees the bigger picture even though we just look through a glass darkly. Little did I realize at this place of the journey, the full impact of the miracles we would have missed if we had not believed that God is a good God and wants the best for us. Jeremiah 29:11 says it best, "For I know the thoughts and plans that I have for you, says the Lord, thoughts and plans for welfare and peace and not for evil, to give you hope in your final outcome.

Debra Young Waller

6

An Example of Faith in Action

What does a person do who was just recently diagnosed with stage four cancer? Does that person sit in a chair and feel sorry for himself? The answer is a definite, 'No'.

We only have one life to live. Every day in self-pity is a day lost to defeat. Where the Bible states in Ephesians 5:16, the Lord knew how to overcome every obstacle that is blocking our path in life. Making the very most of your time [on earth, recognizing and taking advantage of each opportunity and using it with wisdom and diligence], because the days are [filled with] evil. Satan's plan is to 'shut you down'. That's where we have to press toward the goal to win the [Heavenly] prize of the upward call of God in Christ Jesus. Philippians 3:14.

Larry did just what he has always preached, these ways of pressing forward while believing God for their miracle or waiting for an answer to prayer to be manifested in their situations.

After Larry began getting stronger from the hormone therapy treatment, he was able to drive again. His appearance seemed to be almost back to normal. He had several weak moments from the treatment, but he choose to take every day and make the most of each day as he committed his ways unto the Lord.

At A.I.G.A., The Association of International Gospel Assemblies, the organization is a non-profit work. The members are evangelists, teachers and pastors that go through much afflictions due to being on the front line of the battlefield of life. Larry started volunteering in the office of A.I.G.A. When he came into the office, they gave him a desk and he took on his volunteer work as if he was getting paid, even though no salary was given.

Everything he did was as unto the Lord. Colossians 3:23 – Whatever you do [whatever your talk may be], work from the souls [that is, put in your very best effort], as [something done] for the Lord and not for men. Larry would sit at the desk with a large yellow pad of paper and write his notes of every call he made to our members to encourage each call. He wrote the dates he called and a brief note of the conversations with their names.

As I listened from my desk which was right across from his, I could hear words of faith and comfort as he responded to their prayer requests. He prayed over the phone with much fervency. Tears had streamed down his face while he was praying for the members of our organization. After he hung up, frequently he would say, "I feel like we just had church". After about three or four hours later, he would gather up his things and say, "I guess I have to get home now, I'm feeling tired now, I need to rest."

The day was spent with much success as he felt like he accomplished a mission from God. Oh, how I miss hearing him pray for the saints with such love in his heart for others. Larry never missed time spent either on his knees in prayer, reading the Word of God or ministering to others with every opportunity he was given by God. This is truly called, 'A man on a mission'.

Debra Young Waller

7

My Brother's Keeper

Within a few weeks of Larry's diagnosis, my brother, Delbert was also diagnosed with lung cancer. Now, here were two very special men in my life whom I adore going through cancer at the same time. When we are faced with such sudden news of a disease or illness, it is hard to know what to do or who to turn to. Sometimes it's a feeling of isolation as if nobody understands our battle. When we all face such hardships in life, God wastes nothing. Everything can and will be used for a purpose if we just allow ourselves to look past the bad news and put one foot in front of the other.

My brother, Delbert at his home had a family gathering where a group of us were at to encourage him. Delbert had an attack of his emotions which were at that moment overwhelming for him. We all went to his rescue, each one not knowing the best way to approach him to bring encouragement. Then, Delbert made a comment that I'll never forget. "Nobody understands how I feel." He stated. You see, Larry and I had never told anybody other than our sons about Larry's diagnosis. And they only knew of Larry's diagnosis just a few weeks before that day. I looked at Larry and he looked at me. I then spoke up, "Delb, we didn't mention this a few weeks ago, but Larry was diagnosed with cancer too". Delbert looked up as he was sitting on the couch with all of us surrounding him. Delbert looked at me and then looked at Larry standing nearby. There was a surprise look on his face of disbelief and bewilderment. Larry then, shared his story to Delbert as the others listened along with Delbert. Delbert knew that there was someone who did understand his battle.

Larry and Delbert stayed in contact with each other sharing scriptures of healing and spiritual insights that built up each other in the faith. They prayed for each other often and were a strength to each other as they traveled their cancer journey together. Delbert though, in less than six months passed on to be with the Lord. His story of faith and how he reached out to the Lord to draw strength is a story of its own. It's not how we end that's the most important part of our own individual journeys, but it's how well we traveled on the road of life to give God the glory in each and every situation. They were both their Brother's keeper. Now, today, they both are reaping the rewards of what true faith is all about; simple trust in God when we don't understand.

8

Now What, God?

Facing such a transition and uncertainty had me looking at this puzzle that is my life as if I walking in a room where it's completely dark. I am left to see an unclear and incomplete picture. This past year I always felt God with us, the home that we raised our boys in has always been a secure place. I wanted to win the 'Publishers Clearing House' to ease our debts and cancer treatment co-payments. Sure, this is the heart dreaming of a quick answer. And I am a dreamer.

In 2016, there was an overwhelming financial burden we faced because of the accumulation of co-payments we had to pay several times a month.

Me, being the kind of person that has to be a step ahead in my own thinking out of how and when to pay the bills, I was stressed out. Larry and I shared all the responsibilities with our mortgage, electric and a few credit cards. The co-payments I thought were the icing on the cake. These responsibilities had overwhelmed me. Then the unexpected surprise of a letter from the IRS, because of a mistake Medicaid made and we suddenly owed $1,300.00. Okay, now what?

One night I sat on my bed feeling the squeeze of pressure when I kept thinking, What am I gonna do? Lord, what am I going to do now?!

I had that little talk with Jesus, I knew that He heard my every cry. I know the Lord is always with me. God promises in his word he will never leave me nor forsake me. In this desperate moment, I sought him again, "Lord, I feel so overwhelmed right now, I don't know what to do. I can't in myself keep up and Larry can't be burdened with all of this. He can't even go upstairs nor downstairs. Larry can only go in the living room, kitchen and office beside the bathroom. What do I do?

At that very moment, I heard that still small voice just as clear as the light of day, "sell the house". I knew the voice came from my very being, the place where peace rules in our hearts. I knew this voice came from the throne of God. My quick response to the Lord's voice was, "Okay, then, if this is your perfect will, then, let it sell quickly. Otherwise, don't let it sell if this is not your will. Then, let no contract be drawn up and I will take it off the market.

I remembered the word of God that talked about the fleece Gideon made with God. I didn't think I would be in a circumstance where I hit a cross-road to make a fleece.

You see, In the past, Larry and I in those 26 years of living at the log home, had put the home on the market several times, feeling out the perfect will of the Lord.

In those times, we had good intentions of what seemed to be common sense at the time. Larry's good friends from California wanted us to move to California to work with them while they were pastoring a church.

We put the home on the market and searched for a home at a place called, Hesperia, California. For some reason, the home we tried to get a contract on in Hesperia, became unavailable. Our home in DeSoto, Missouri didn't sell after being on the market for a year. We assumed at this point, God didn't want us to sell. So, we took the home off the market.

Another time when we put the log home on the market was when the pastors from Lubbock, Texas wanted us to work with them in ministry. Larry's mother was planning to move in with us. She was living in Southern California and wanted to be with us, but at the same time not be too far from her other sons.

Again, we were pursuing a home in Lubbock, Something with the contract didn't work out and our home in DeSoto, Missouri didn't sell after being on the market for another year. Later on in the near future, Larry's mother passed away.

Thank goodness the Lord sometimes says, 'No'. If we would have sold our home at those times, history would have been altered in our lives. Little did we at those times realize one day Larry would be diagnosed with stage four cancer. We could not have known how God would use all our family and church family to uphold our weary arms as we fought the battle of terminal illness even though everyday we did believe in miracles. We did believe with God that all things are possible.

Needless to say, we, within a week got a contract on the log home where we'd had our homestead for 26 years. This home being on the market for only one week, was nothing short of a miracle! Within one week we were signing the papers to be out of the house within less than three weeks from signing this contract.

Getting a contract so quickly was extremely sudden with no time to even figure out the details of where we would go from there? I though, knew the Lord was steering us to a better place financially. I also knew God is not the Author of confusion and He is not into demoting his children. I reached out and choose to take hold of his invisible hand. I'm reminded in the Bible, Isaiah 42:16 which says, "And I will bring the blind by a way that they know not; I will lead them in paths that they have not known: I will make darkness light before them, and crooked things straight. These things will I do unto them, and not forsake them."

Faith is not faith until it is put to the test. We never know when we follow the Lord how long this journey will take, nor how deep the darkness will get when we choose to follow Him.

9

Then, Suddenly, an Unexpected Miracle

Life is about timing, and timing is everything. Our times are in his hands. Psalms 31:15.

This new day of adventure left us now with, where do we go to live from here? We have to not only find a home but, be moved in within three weeks away. I contacted a real estate agent not knowing where to start. I also, searched on the internet for homes that were for sale. We needed a home where we could get out of debt. A place we could call home.

I found a home on-line at Wildwood lake subdivision where the home was a bank foreclosure. This home was low budget with a little bit of country. While Larry and I were peeking through the window of this house that was two minutes from the log house, a woman called out to us from across the street. She had introduced herself as Marilyn. She told us that she was a semi-retired real estate agent and that she could let us in to look around. After looking around, I couldn't help but think this isn't the house we were meant to buy. Larry started saying that he needed to go to the bathroom, and with prostate cancer, when he needs to go it's an emergency.

After we explained everything to her, she told us to go to the house on the corner across the street. As we were walking over, she mentioned to us how she and her husband were fixing it up to resell. They originally bought it for their daughter but didn't feel it was right for her. As soon as we walked in, we both felt like this was home! While Larry was using the restroom, I felt compelled to make an offer on a house that wasn't even on the market yet.

By the grace of God, I pressed past the 'What if she thinks I am crazy?' I blurted out to her, "Marilyn, I know you just met us, but as I told you earlier how Larry is going through his cancer treatments and we got a contract four days ago on our log house. We have three weeks to find a new home and move out. I feel led by the Lord to make a crazy offer of $45,000 in cash after we get paid from the closing on our home?"

Marilyn looked a little surprised gave me a big smile, after thinking for a moment, she told me that she would need to talk to her husband, and she would get back to me. As Marilyn and I were sharing our numbers, Larry came walking out of the restroom with a smile on his face. I'm sure he had heard our conversation. The very next day, Marilyn and her husband, Bruce, called us with a counteroffer of $50,000. They said the house needs a new roof, and they still had to finish putting the flooring in. They finally agreed on $46,000 with the promise that we would replace the roof within a month.

Now, you can't tell me this wasn't a divine appointment set by our God. They had no idea if our words meant anything, but they stepped out and took us at our word. Years ago you would hear of a hand shake was as good as your word. Now days, things are different. People just don't trust each other like they used to. So many people go back on their word which has in time, annulled that type of hand shake contract.

We knew at the moment over the phone conversation, we had a divine contract that only God could have set-up. This indeed, has been another miracle on the cancer journey.

During these few weeks before we were able to close on our log home and close on our soon to be new home, by faith, volunteered to help work on the home on Wildwood.

Praise God that our sons were able to work with us in preparing this new home to move in soon. They helped us by putting in the laminate hard wood flooring which Bruce and Marilyn had already purchased for the home. James, our youngest son put in one floor and Jacob our oldest son put in another bedroom. Things were coming together quickly while at home I spent the early mornings before work and late in the evenings after work packing things in boxes to be moved.

On this cancer journey something else developed as another miracle. Marilyn and Bruce, the owners of the home in Wildwood that we were soon to close on, spoke up and offered for us to go on and move our things in to beat the deadline of the closing which was less than three weeks away. This is a true work of God when the log home hadn't even been closed on and, Wildwood, the soon to be new home was still in contract. With God, all things are possible to him who believes. The Lord has been orchestrating again every detail of the transition to work for our good. Jeremiah 29:11-13, "For I know the thoughts and plans that I have for you, says the Lord, thoughts and plans for welfare and peace and not for evil, to give you hope in your final outcome." This scripture is placed throughout this book to help you understand, you are never alone.   God has the bigger picture and desires to bless us while he's teaching us how to trust and lean on him.

'We have less than three weeks,' kept running through my brain. Again, after spending time in prayer, I cast my cares upon the Lord. My heart knew God had the answers to how to move in quickly when Larry was in no way able to do any moving because of his medical condition.   At this time on the cancer journey, he had to use a cane.

Just as the Lord had been faithful before, he gave me a battle plan! Every week a few days before the weekend God instructed me to post on Facebook to our friends the plan.   This is a scriptural strategy from the Bible; Habakkuk 2, "Then the Lord answered me and said, "Write the vision and engrave it plainly on [clay] tablets so that the one who reads it will run."

I posted on Facebook the plan to move. Within the next three weekends we desperately need help moving into our next home after selling our log home. Please contact me as soon as possible." We received an over-whelming reply. Each week there was enough help to move everything.

When the first weekend came, I knew in my heart we were moving into a smaller home. The log home had three levels of stuff with three sheds outside to clear out as well. "Okay Lord, now what do I do?" I cried out as I stood in the front yard of the log home. Again, I heard God's still small voice say, "Give away the things you don't need or value like personal mementos".

When the men and women came to help us, they knew this cancer journey had put a strain on our finances. None of those who came ever mentioned pay or compensation for their help. I immediately responded to the Lord's direction given to me.

The men and women asked me and Larry who stood by with his cane in his hand as he leaned on it for support, what they should do with each thing from the sheds. I spoke up with Larry's approval, as I pointed at the things that I knew in my heart to let go of, "Take it and give it away to someone." Now, there was also a man who owned a second-hand store down south who I believe helped others with the proceeds of sales from his little store. We let him take several truck loads with him. We knew the Lord made a way to not only to bless others, but also find a solution to getting rid of the things that we couldn't take with us for lack of room.

One week we had those from 'Just around the corner' flooring business volunteer. Another week was a few men and their family members from 'Boeing'. The other week was friends and relatives. Throughout the week, my best friends, Charlotte, Judy, Wesley Waller and Pat as well as other family stepped in and helped me move boxes.

The days of closing on the log home and closing at Wildwood (the new home) were back to back, as we signed the papers. This event had been bitter-sweet. We definitely had a beautiful home to go to as we walked away from the home we had spent over 26 years in raising our two sons.

After the log home sold; we were debt free. We found a home that Larry could navigate with ease and something we could afford on one salary. Every day I would hope and pray for the manifestation of his physical healing. There were times when I would sit and wonder, why isn't God sitting me down and telling me his plan? Why does Larry have to go through this?

After we moved in our new home in August of 2016, at the end of the month, we kept our word and put a new roof on the house. The Lord worked it out to where we had enough money to keep our word to Marilyn and Bruce.

10

The Miracle List

After all expenses were paid on the home and the new roof, I had enough to fulfill a list of things I wanted for the new home. I felt like I just gave up something much bigger and meaningful, so I made a list of a few things I asked the Lord for in exchange. Again, God made a way without paying the full price for anything I asked for on this list.

The things I put on this list were, #1: A specific bed, #2: a big screen television, #3: an electric fireplace, #4: a lift chair for Larry and later we added #5: a camper trailer for him to go back on the road after his manifestation of healing we expected from the beginning of the cancer journey.

#1 MIRACLE: My Full size bed had been around since 1990. This at one time was such a beautiful first bed my first husband, the late Patrick Fortner, had bought right after we built the log home. The brass bed had served its purpose throughout the years but, now, was falling apart and scuffed in discreet places. We bought the bed just two months before Patrick was killed in a truck accident five minutes away from the home. Later, I married Rev. Larry Young and went on the road with him.

My detailed description was big wood posts, black iron rail trim and a queen size bed. I began looking through the Facebook Marketplace of buy, sell and trade after I prayed. The bed I asked the Lord for popped up on the site for around $175.00! This bed also served a purpose to win a soul for the Lord. Proverbs 11:30, "The fruit of the [consistently] righteous is a tree of life. And he who is wise captures and wins souls [for God – he gathers them for eternity]."

My Sons and I went to buy the bed from a private owner. The owner of the bed lived over an hour away on a long rough gravel and dirt road back in the woods. When we got there, a woman who had a wrap over her head answered the door. She seemed frail and very pale. She let us in and led us to the bedroom where the bed was located. We didn't buy the mattress, just the bed and frame. She shared with me her life story of her battle with cancer while my sons proceeded to take down the bed to load into the truck.

After the boys loaded the bed into the truck, they came back into the house to walk me out. When I had paid the woman for the bed, I then shared with her our story briefly about Larry's cancer journey up to this point. You see, when someone is going through something and you have a testimony to share of how God assisted you on your journey with faith, and how much God loves you and strengthened you, then, you can relate and they know you understand their battle.

As I felt the unction of the Lord, I continued to share the plan of salvation. "Ma'am, would you like to received Jesus Christ who loves you very much and wants to give you strength like he has given us strength to go through this cancer journey?" She smiled with a look in her eyes of hope and excitement with an anxious tone she replied back, "Yes, I would like to". As I took her frail hand, me, Jake and James bowed our heads and I led her in prayer to receive Christ.

If we hadn't gone through this journey with Larry, this would not have ever happened. For everything there is a season and a time for every purpose under heaven. Ecclesiastes 3 states it well. God knows how to make sweet lemonade out of the lemons in life. This is one desire God gave me on my list I presented to the Lord, a queen size wood post with iron trim bed with a purpose.

#2 MIRACLE: I requested to the Lord on my list was an electric wood look with podium fireplace. I looked again on the Facebook Marketplace buy, sell and trade. The fireplace came up to view. The Lord again, gave it to me from a local private person. When Larry would get a chill, he would have the option to turn on the fireplace and draw warmth in the room.

#3 MIRACLE: I added to the list, a Burgundy lift chair for Larry. I realized these are very expensive and knew I needed to save as much extra to continue to keep up with expenses. After I asked the Lord to help us get a good lift chair, I went online again, to the Marketplace on Facebook, buy, sell and trade. There was the lift chair but for around $400.00. I sent the requested offer of $200.00 for the Burgundy lift chair and briefed the people of Larry's condition.

A day went by and still no response. The people hadn't even viewed my offer. I prayed again but, another day went by. "Lord", I said, "What's going on? I know in my heart this chair is from you." After sharing with my friend what was going on, she suggested that maybe these people are away to a place where they aren't receiving phone service. Another day went by. I made up my mind I will not give up. God will work this out. My faith had to be assisted with patience which has it's perfect work in my heart. Hebrews 6:12 explains this well, "That ye be not slothful, but followers of them who through faith and patience inherit the promises. Sometimes people give up right before their miracle. When I prayed I believed I would receive but, if I had given up I would have lost my blessing right at the midnight hour. This was a lesson of faith through patience.

I checked the internet site again to see if there was a response. This time, they responded and explained they were away on a trip and had no phone service. They accepted my offer of $200.00. We went after the chair with help and now, Larry had a lift chair to help him get up and down. Larry and all of us were encouraged on this cancer journey as we witnessed the Lord walking with us every step of the way!

Now, right after we brought home the fireplace, our sweet Larry sat down as he looked at the fireplace and said with a big smile on his face, "This is so therapeutic". We all looked at each other with Satisfaction we all were able to help him be more comfortable on his cancer journey. Larry was physically battling with the pain in his bones. Since the diagnosis was cancer in the bones and lymph nodes, he had his good day and his bad days. We were relieved when he had a good day but, if he overdid it that day, the next day he was in much pain and struggled getting off the couch so between the warmth of the fireplace and the lift chair, we saw the look on Larry's face of gratitude and appreciation as he continued to encourage us with his words of faith.

#4 MIRACLE: The item now, was a huge big screen television. I followed the same pattern to look for the TV and the Lord led me to another divine appointment. Larry, myself and a close friend, Wesley Waller took the truck to the next town to go buy and pick up the television which was sold to me for $175.00. The price of this was such a miracle for a television which worked perfect. While Larry waited in the truck because of the fatigue he was dealing with, Wes and I went inside the house to settle business. The purpose God had in mind was when I went inside to get pay for the television, a young girl was living with her mother. She was an unwed mother with a very young beautiful child trying to raise money to regroup in her life. She shared her story that her boyfriend got her pregnant and hired someone to cause her to fall down stairs to end the pregnancy. As she opened her heart up to me, she had a sense of safety with a peace knowing in her heart I would understand. I believe we are Christ Ambassadors as in 2 Corinthians 5:20, being sent out to heirs of salvation.

I felt what the Lord felt for this young lady, a heart of compassion. After she shared with me her story, I asked her if I could pray for her. She immediately said, yes and let me know she was a new Christian. The Lord wanted her to be reminded that he is with her and brought me to bring her encouragement as others in the past had encouraged me. I prayed for her as the tears streamed down her face, God confirmed his word with His anointing. She felt the presence of the Lord as he confirmed to her how real he is. She just received a visitation of the Lord.

Once the mission from God was complete, Wes then, helped me bring home my miracle from the Lord. I felt like I just had church. Where two or more are gathered in his name, he is in the midst of them. Matthew 18:20.

#5 MIRACLE: Now, the last on our list was definitely a group effort to bring to Larry's attention of hope for his future evangelistic adventures. He desired an RV trailer to travel like he did for so many years before, as he shared the good news of the Gospel of Jesus Christ.

Larry and I prayed in the name of Jesus for the Lord to make a way when there seemed to be no way. Larry, the man of faith, all of a sudden received a creative idea! My dear husband exclaimed excitedly, "I'm going to call my minister friends and share my vision as in the word that says in Habakkuk 2:2, "Write the vision, and make it plain upon tables, that he may run that readeth it." Larry did just that. He began calling those ministers that in the past stood with him as he had stood with them in ministry. The response was overwhelming.

Miracles on the Cancer Journey

I, at the same time, began once again, checking out the Facebook Marketplace, buy, sell and trade. I found a 24 foot camper trailer. The price was negotiable so I put in a bid for around $1,200.00. We got the camper trailer. Now, to go pick it up and pay for it.

Jake, my son, his wife, Josie with baby Cheyla in the back seat and our dear friend, Wesley Waller, all took a very long ride to go pick up the blessing from the Lord, a 24 foot camper trailer. Larry was ecstatic about this answer to prayer. He pressed forward to his future and chose to not look back.

On the way back with the camper trailer, we were close to five minutes away from home when suddenly the camper trailer had a blow out on one of the tires. We just happened to be right by Saint Frances State Park and pulled over immediately. Everyone was safe, but stranded without a way to change the tire on the camper. We all began to pray and God heard us. A man pulled up within minutes to assist us. This man had what we needed to help us. Within a short while, in the heat of the day, they changed the tire. Here is another miracle on the cancer journey. The Lord answers before we call and while we are yet speaking he will hear. Isaiah 65:24. We were at the right place at the right time as well as the man who helped us. Only God could have done this intervention of help.

Debra Young Waller

11

Metastases to the Brain? Now You See It Now You Don't

October 2016, it was beginning to get a bit chilly outside. Larry had pain in his body more frequently now. Here we did all we knew to do to keep him comfortable while waiting for our manifestation of healing. We did believe with God all things are possible and we did believe in the promises of God. We had friends that came to visit from Oregon, Bob, Larry's long-time friend, and one of Larry's brothers came from California. They all came to give encouragement to us all. During this visit, Larry hit his head on the shed door while they were looking at the lawn mower which hadn't been working right. His pain level not only in his neck increased, but all over. He was enduring much pain throughout his body.

I observed the symptoms Larry was dealing with and I pondered in my heart, I knew that something was not right. We made an appointment with the doctor at the Cancer Treatment Center.

After much testing, one of the doctors came up with a diagnosis by x-ray. It appeared there was cancer that had spread to the brain. Again, we sat together in the tiny room where me, our dear best friend Judy sat along with the doctor and Larry. While the doctor was sharing the bad report, the look on our faces were of shock and disbelief. But, after a few moments, Larry spoke up. His words were nothing but a mini sermon of faith filled words. Judy and I along with the doctor listened with surprise on our faces. Only the Lord could have given the grace for Larry to share what God had put deep within his spirit, the spoken Word of God coming out of him like a flowing river to refresh the souls of the hearer.

The doctor ordered more testing at the hospital near us. As times before on this cancer journey, we waited for the call from the doctor to give us the results again. Everybody we could contact prayed fervently while we waited. Then, the call came to give us the test results. Where the radiologist found spots of cancer, the new x-rays showed up with nothing to show! Only God. Only God could have changed this.

12

The Last Diagnosis, Treatment No Longer Working

Time went by and Larry at this point was at a place where he was doing great. Then, in a short while later, he began more frequently crying out in pain, walking the floor and crying out to God in prayer. We all jumped up immediately and began praying the promises of God with him. Within an hour or so, the pain subsided. Larry was taking pain medication ordered from the Doctor, but it seemed to not be helping. Larry also, began to lose weight. We set another appointment to see the doctor. The doctor, again, called us in his office; he looked at us both and said with deep concern in his eyes, the hormone therapy isn't working anymore. Every time usually each year since 2014 when Larry started cancer treatment of hormone therapy, the doctor prescribed a different hormone therapy. Within a few weeks of starting a new type of hormone therapy, Larry would put the weight back on and regain his strength.

The Doctor continued to speak, but not the words I was prepared to hear. *"There is no more treatment for you. We've done all that we can do."* "Ok, now what, Lord", I prayed in my heart. My thoughts afterward came up with the conclusion, "Now, it's time

Debra Young Waller

for Larry's miracle to be manifested!" So, faith must be tested or it isn't faith." This was my conclusion. I proclaimed this to Larry and we both agreed to that statement of faith.

13

Christmas Day, the Day Ezekiel Left Us

Finally, it was Christmas! This is the time when family comes together and share the joy of giving. The time when we have our annual Christmas party with singing and rejoicing as we celebrate the birth of our Savior, Jesus Christ, who was born to die to save the lost.

Every year, at our annual Christmas Party, we all joined in with the song, "The twelve days of Christmas". Larry wore his Santa Clause hat with pride and he had a sparkle in his eyes when he belted out his favorite part 'five golden rings' almost mimicking the pictures displayed of Santa Clause. I video taped our group Christmas song as we all sat in a circle with family and friends in 2016, not knowing, this would be the last Christmas celebration we would have with with Larry. We enjoyed and cherished our Christmas celebration with our close family and friends! What a fun time we all had!

Now, Christmas day had arrived. This year our special day fell on a Sunday! Larry and I got ready in our Christmas best to head to church for a Christmas Service, we were all ready to go the door when the phone rang. Our oldest son, Jacob called saying that tragedy had struck, instead of our Christmas service at church, we were headed to the hospital. Many prayer warriors came to pray for our grandson Ezekiel to be born on earth, sadly, he was born into heaven. God welcomed Ezekiel Morton Young into heaven on Christmas Day. As much as this hurt our hearts and we, as a family we're devastated, the Bible says in Proverbs 3:5 "Trust in the Lord with all thine heart; and lean not unto thine own understanding."

Ezekiel was Larry's namesake, the fifth generation to carry the name Morton. Larry was devastated, and this truly began the deterioration of his physical body. The prayer warriors prayed for peace and comfort in a time of complete devastation. I did my best to comfort them In this time of need.

Larry who was Ezekiel's Grandpa, spoke softly with immense sorrow said, "No, No, Ezekiel is the one that is supposed to carry my name!"

Larry came home to lay down and try to understand this terrible thing that had shaken our family. Our close friends Jack and Paula Morgan came to comfort Larry while I stayed at the hospital trying to comfort our son Jacob and his wife, Josie.

The strength of our beautiful daughter in law, Josie, had to have came straight from God. I have never witnessed such admirable grace as what had carried her and Jacob in such a hot fire of affliction. This experience had such a witness of faith that carried the bond of love for God as they trusted Him even in the fire of hardship and grief to the highest level. There were no words to express this gut wrenching and helpless feeling that gripped the soul.

Our faith remains by the grace of God, we will be together again. Until we meet again Ezekiel, until we meet again. 2 Corinthians 5:6-8 "Therefore we are always confident, knowing that, whilst we are at home in the body, we are absent from the Lord:(For we walk by faith, not by sight:) We are confident, I say, and willing rather to be absent from the body, and to be present with the Lord.

Hebrews 11:6 has an entirely new meaning now, "But without faith it is impossible to please him". I always believed when the word speaks on faith, it means believe what you pray for will happen no matter what. What I didn't take into account was, sometimes there is more involved in our prayers that our mind doesn't comprehend. Sometimes God says "No". Sometimes, God says "this is for a greater purpose." Faith in this circumstance is the kind of faith that simply trusts in God's love and knows God has a plan for each one of our lives.

Josie and Jake demonstrated the purest form of 'faith in the raw', when you trust God, even when you don't understand. They proved to the world how much they love their Heavenly Father and how God will carry them through the valley of the shadow of death.

Psalm 23:4 "Even though I walk through the valley of the shadow of death, I fear no evil, for you are with me; your rod to protect and your staff to guide, they comfort and console me."

I'm sure when Stephen in the Bible was being stoned to death, his faith was not shaken nor did his love for God fail. He knew the Lord loved him deeply, but also understood that Ecclesiastes 3, "In everything there is a season and a time for every purpose under heaven."

Stephen in Acts 7:55, "Being full of the Holy Spirit and led by Him, gazed into heaven and saw the Glory the great splendor and majesty of God, and Jesus standing at the right hand of God."

Stephen walked with God like Jake and Josie all of their lives, walk daily with God as well. They displayed tender hearts through broken by grief. The Lord now, was taking them both with their daughter, Cheyla, through the valley of the shadow of death.

The Lord came to heal the broken-hearted and binds up their wounds [healing their pain and comforting their sorrow]. God did not forsake them, but for a special purpose allowed pain and sorrow, but joy comes in the morning.

I will never forget the unshakable love that was demonstrated that day by our loved ones and during the weeks to come as Ezekiel was laid to rest, and to you all, we say 'Thank You', your generosity and love will never be forgotten.

Miracles on the Cancer Journey

Weeks later, as I was scrolling through Facebook, I saw pictures of someone's family posing with a new-born baby. Flashes of our Christmas day flooded my mind but soon I refocused on God's promises where those who are in Christ Jesus will one day be with him for eternity. We don't have to understand why God allows terrible things to happen to good people, we just need to stand in faith, and simply trust in His plan.

I heard someone say, "The depth of the pain in life usually indicates the height you will attain in the next season of your life." I choose to believe this.

After Jake was born, we conceived again, my daughter, Jackqueline Michelle. Three months into the pregnancy, she was taken to heaven. God let me conceive again, my son, James.

I know that I will see my grand-babies again, Ezekiel and Bennet. Bennet is my grandchild that was taken to heaven in the twelfth week of gestation.

Debra Young Waller

14

A Curve in the Road, Hospice

With Larry taking a slight turn for the worst, we felt like our lives had been turned upside down. This had us starting the process for the in-home hospice program. The decision to bring hospice in was inspired by me not being able to be home to care for Larry. His medicines were multiplying on the tray while he continued getting weaker with more medical issues.

I remember the doctors diagnosing my brother Delbert around the same time as Larry in 2013. He died in hospice within six months of his diagnosis. We still didn't know how God was going to turn this around, but the still small voice became clearer in my heart when I remembered the word of God telling us in Isaiah 30:21 "Your ears will hear a word behind you, This is the way, walk in it, whenever you turn to the right or the left."

But, it would be on our terms with he and myself standing, in faith, on the promises of God. Larry and I prayed together for the right nurse, the right team while me and my family watched out for Larry with a keen eye on the situation.

When we finally got our first visit from his nurse, Jennifer, she told us about the options hospice offered like music therapy, a home-health nurse aide as well as getting Jennifer twice a week. Larry and I were ecstatic to find out that she was a Spirit-filled Christian. It comforted us knowing that she understood where we stood, that trusting God comes first in our cancer journey. I knew there was a plan from God that involved the hospice program. Out of all the nurses we could have gotten; she was a born-again and Spirit-filled Christian, and we found out she was connected to our daughter-in-law, Josie.

After getting Larry officially signed up with hospice, I showed her a video of our granddaughter, Cheyla. She was dancing with her piano music in the living room. A few days later she saw the same video when, Josie, was visiting her grandpa. She saw the video and got excited, exclaimed she had seen this somewhere else! After putting the dots together, Jennifer said, "I believe God put both men in my life." Little do we realize when the Lord is directing us like pieces of a puzzle fitly joined together to create a divine picture painted by God. "A man's mind plans his way [as he journeys through life], But the LORD directs his steps and establishes them." Proverbs 16:9

15

Divine Rays of Sunshine

The following weekend was like a breath of fresh air. I needed to go to the post office to mail a bill that was almost late. I wasn't sure if Larry would feel up to making a run into town, but I asked him anyway. One thing led to another after the post office; we got a soda from the drive thru, we shopped at Dollar General and Goodwill, visited my mom and stopped to get lunch at Dairy Queen. The way we were laughing and talking this was a moment in time when we got to enjoy each other's company. For a moment in time, we forgot about the cancer journey and enjoyed the rays of sunshine we were having with each other. We didn't just look like husband and wife, but best friends.

The way the sun was shining and warming us, it almost felt like the Lord was telling us to enjoy the gift of life. Later that day my oldest son, Jake, came over with his wife, Josie, and their daughter Cheyla. Then my youngest son, James, came strolling in with his new girlfriend, Heather. What a perfect way to continue the day! We had fun hanging out at the house, while the kids were playing a game with bursts of laughter. We were all joking and carrying on, when out of nowhere Larry started feeling crushing pain.

Debra Young Waller

16

The Fight of Faith, The Battle in My Mind

My mind snapped back to the reality of his suffering and pain. Larry had been doing so good for the past three days. Larry's pain level had been so low we almost forgot that he was sick. We immediately went into prayer over him, and then used the pain medication to help combat the cancerous symptoms. It was two days of dealing with the nausea that the pain medication caused and the pain from the cancer symptoms, even though, he was still standing firmly on the promises of God.

My mind would sometimes wander in a fleshly direction, swaying me from the promises of God. I would realize that this is not the voice of God, but an attack from the enemy. This voice brings tormenting fear and doubt to my mind. When I realize it isn't the voice of God, the Holy Spirit reminds me of the scripture I need. God's word has been hidden in my heart. "Your word I have treasured and stored in my heart that I may not sin against you." Psalm 119:11.

His word says that "But He was wounded for our transgressions, He was crushed for our wickedness [our sin, our injustice, our wrongdoing]; the punishment [required] for our well-being fell on Him, and by His stripes (wounds) we are healed." Isaiah 53:5.

75

When the enemy comes and attacks our thoughts, the word tells us in 2 Corinthians 10:5 "We are destroying sophisticated arguments and every exalted and proud thing that sets itself up against the [true] knowledge of God, and we are taking every thought and purpose captive to the obedience of Christ."

This is a process, there was a war going on in my mind. God kept speaking to my spirit about keeping my armor of protection on. "Therefore, put on the complete armor of God, so that you will be able to [successfully] resist and stand your ground in the evil day [of danger], and having done everything [that the crisis demands], to stand firm [in your place, fully prepared, immovable, victorious]. Ephesians 6:13.

For years we were a team in the ministry, we would hold meetings to encourage the church. We reminded them when prayer is brought before the Lord, we stand in faith expecting. I am grateful that the Lord had prepared me for the hardest battle of our life. Now we were going on three years of being in the fire, but we were staying in prayer, claiming the promises, singing in exhortation and preaching the word of God. We still believe that with God all things are possible.

One thing I have learned through this journey is, don't give up, keep believing and hoping. I rest knowing God loves us. When He seems silent remember that the teacher is always silent during the test. We must remember that God's word does not return void.

"For as the rain and the snow come down from heaven, and do not return there without watering the earth, making it bear and sprout, and providing seed to the sower and bread to the eater, so will My word be which goes out of My mouth; it will not return to Me void (useless, without result), without accomplishing what I desire, and without succeeding in the matter for which I sent it." Isaiah 55:10-11.

Debra Young Waller

17

The Prayer Warriors; My Dream Team

I awoke to Larry sitting in his lift chair; he looked so lifeless and pale! I sprung into action, checking his blood pressure, it was extremely low. When he told me how bad his pain was on top of his blood pressure, I called our pastor and my uncle, Carl McKalip and immediately went into prayer over Larry. Then we, thankfully, were able to get a hold of Jennifer, Larry's Hospice Nurse. She was at the house within thirty minutes and immediately got things rolling to regroup his medication.

Jennifer also thought it would be better for him if we got a hospital bed. When the bed arrived, we got him set up in the living room. Jennifer also made a call to have the nurse's aide come more often with a hospice volunteer. I gave a call to our dear family in Christ, Tom and Carolyn, asking them to sit with Larry while I was at work. They immediately responded to the need with action. Thank God for His children who answer the call of being a blessing! I call these amazing, caring people, my dream team. Each and every person on this cancer team mentioned in this book has played a part and was strategically placed in our lives by God.

"So then, while we [as individual believers] have the opportunity, let us do good to all people [not only being helpful, but also doing that which promotes their spiritual well-being], and especially [being a blessing] to those of the household of faith (born-again believers). Galatians 6:10 gives us all the instructions how to serve each other with the bond of unity. This is the foundation by which ministries are birthed from. We are all called to serve as unto the Lord. God will always, throughout our lives, present and unfold opportunities to serve. Jesus was our perfect example when he washed the disciple's feet.

This is showing the love of God in a practical way. I will never forget all of those who were then and are now the hand of God reaching out to my family in this time of need. I believe miracles happen every day, big and small. I choose to see God in the simple acts of kindness, like a passing smile exchanged in the store. Some have answered the call to help us when I prayed, and one day it will be my turn to answer someone else's call when they need it.

Soon, Larry seemed to be doing much better. Jennifer really knew her stuff! God is so good to us; He gave us the right professionals and Christian influences. God knows how to communicate to us without using words. Sometimes it feels like He is being silent, until someone shows me the love of God.

When others reach out whether it's their love and concern or them stopping and praying for us, God always knows when to send His children who are listening to reach out to us. This is well beyond our control, but my God is mightier than our circumstances. This reminds me of Joshua, he fought the battle and continued victoriously as long as Moses held his staff up before God. When his arms got tired he had the right people around him, great men of God who helped hold his arms up!

We are surrounded by people who love us and the Lord. Those who are grounded in the word are holding us up in prayer and showering us with words of encouragement. The fervent prayer of a righteous man gives us a great advantage!

"Now when Moses held up his hand, Israel prevailed, and when he lowered his hand [due to fatigue], Amalek prevailed. But Moses' hands were heavy and he grew tired. So they took a stone and put it under him, and he sat on it. Then Aaron and Hur held up his hands, one on one side and one on the other side; so it was that his hands were steady until the sun set." Exodus 17:11-12. We all need moral support among other means of support when we go through the storms of our lives. Everybody has a ministry to fulfill. As long as we have breath, we as God's creation have the ability to strengthen the faith of each other. To encourage one another in the Lord.

Debra Young Waller

18

Salvation Victory in the Parking Lot

Early one Friday evening, Larry wanted to treat me on a date. Going on a date was something we did often before he was diagnosed with stage four cancer. Little do we realize when we get an idea to do something, it was actually an inspired idea from the Lord to set us up to be used for His glory.

Larry was already dressed and ready to go when I walked into the house after working at the office all day. What a refreshing sight to see him all excited and full of energy.

We had such a wonderful time talking about good things and great plans for our future. Though Larry wasn't able to eat much, the quality time together was priceless as we created memories that would last a life time.

When we went up to the counter to pay for our food, the cashier took a very long time waiting on us. It seemed like their priorities at that moment seemed more important than taking our money. Patience in this matter was important to not get agitated. I looked at Larry who was beginning to balance himself with his walker. He still wanted to be the man and stand at the counter to pay as he had done so many times before.

Thank you Lord for giving me the spirit of self-control or else I may have given the cashier a verbal piece of my mind. I remembered the scripture that says, "Be swift to hear, slow to speak and slow to wrath, James 1:19.

Sometimes these things are a test of faith or that we may be detained for a reason. At the time though, I didn't think about this. I only trusted that maybe there's something else going on here. I didn't want to say something that I'd regret later. Finally, the cashier decided to wait on us, by then, it was beginning to get late, and I don't like to drive a night.

I proceeded to help Larry get into the passenger side of the car. Then, I folded up the walker and opened up the back door to slide the walker on the back seat. I suddenly noticed a woman who was about in her late thirties, standing by the curb patiently waiting for me to shut the car door.

I spoke up apologetically, "Ma'am, I'm sorry I'm in your way." I'm almost done here. She responded back at me with a gentle, compassionate tone, "Oh, that's quite okay, I understand, is he your Grandpa?" Well, I definitely was taken back some with that comment. I hadn't realized during this cancer journey how frail Larry had become and how much the treatments had taken their toll on his outward appearance.

Miracles on the Cancer Journey

I exclaimed, "No, he's my husband." Life just happens without any notice, then, as children of God, we take one day at a time while we stand on the promises of God, during this journey, we were put on display by God to represent his amazing grace as he strengthened our inner being. This stranger had touched a very sensitive place in my heart that triggered emotions of vulnerability while giving me an opportunity to 'share our story'. Now, I fully understood why we were detained for so long at the restaurant counter, 'for such a time as this'.

She felt a bit of embarrassment and explained, "I apologize, I didn't know that he is your husband". She felt she had offended me, but it was the opposite, I had a new door of opportunity to share the reason we have hope. She introduced herself as Holly and began asking questions about Larry's diagnosis. I began sharing our story to Holly and how God had given us the peace that passes all understanding. Holly opened up to me briefly as she shared what she was going through in her life.

One thing I had learned in life, your testimony is the power behind your ministry. When you've been through hardship, you are now equipped to bear other's burdens and sympathize with their battles.

Holly came back with a question of why do bad things happen to good people. Now, as I in my heart prayed for the Lord to give me wisdom in this conversation, He took hold of the reigns as I simply just opened my mouth and let God fill my words with His wisdom. "We don't focus on the why's but that we have a personal relationship with Jesus Christ, our Lord. He paid the price at the cross of Calvary and He is walking through this cancer journey with us. One day, we will be with Jesus for eternity, because now, our names are written in the Lambs book of life. This earth is full of disease and corruption, but one day we will forever be with him in heaven where there is no disease neither sickness, nor pain. This is the reason why we have peace that passes all understanding. It's not a religion, but a relationship with our Lord and Savior, Jesus Christ who is alive and well and lives within our heart."

I could feel the presence of the Lord and his anointing as I spoke to Holly. She was saturated with the Holy Spirit as He touched her heart. I knew God was using me and Larry in a mighty way to set the captive free. I, then, as I was led by the Holy Spirit, proceeded to take the conversation to the next level of God's perfect plan for our date night adventure.

I gave the question to Holly like many times before as the Lord worked with me. "Holly, would you like to know Jesus in this personal way as we do?; would you like to ask Jesus into your heart to be the Lord of your life and have him walk with you too on your journey of life?" Immediately, Holly responded, she didn't even hesitate but, eagerly said, "Yes, I would like to do that, what do I do? What do I say?" I then with so much joy and excitement led Holly in the Sinner's prayer. A new name was written in Glory, her name now is written in the Lamb's book of Life!. This to me, is the greatest miracle of all! The mission from God is one less soul in hell, one more soul for heaven. This is how the Lord feels about salvation, Proverbs 11:30, "The fruit of the [consistently] righteous is a tree of life. And he who is wise captures and wins souls [for God-he gathers them for eternity]."

Holly and I hugged each other with a sincere heart. Then, reluctantly, went our separate ways, me in the driver's seat of my car to take Larry home and Holly in her car with her new life, living for the Lord. This is where faith comes in when God saves a soul, He knows how to follow up with others who not only plant the word, but also water the seed that has been planted. The miracle of God has a way of helping each one of us to stay on track. That's why we should always continue praying for one another, thus fulfilling the will of the Lord.

After I buckled in my seat belt, I glanced over to the side window at Holly's car, we both locked eyes as a well-planned event by God just took place. Now, Holly was on her own great adventure in life while the Lord ordered her footsteps 'for such a time as this'.

I began sharing with Larry what had just happened outside of the car as he had waited patiently for me this whole time. He knew in his spirit, God was orchestrating this whole day from the time we left, to the grand event of a parking lot meeting place where miracles happen. Larry was just as excited as I was to know we both were once again, a team in ministry with God working in us. Philippians 2:13 says, "For it is [not your strength, but it is] God who is effectively at work in you, both to will and to work [that is, strengthening, energizing, and creating in you the longing and the ability to fulfill your purpose] for His good pleasure."

19

The Surprise Birthday Party for Larry

The next morning after mine and Larry's miracle date night, Larry had physically taken a plunge. He struggled immensely as he tried to get out of bed. I gave him some yogurt, a light breakfast to prepare him for his morning medications. This was the day Josie and the others worked hard to have a surprise birthday party for Larry to encourage him. Every birthday for the past three years had been a miracle hurdle he had jumped through by faith. My job was to get Larry up and dressed for this special occasion, then we were to get him into the car with his walker.

Larry complained he just didn't feel up to going anywhere and wanted to be left alone. I had to get him at the church's fellowship hall by 12:00p.m. I knew the people who were invited would be waiting on us anticipating Larry's arrival. The birthday guests had been there since 11:00 a.m. Larry in his medical condition had expressed he was hurting this day and not feeling well. In one sense I felt bad to have to push him to go anywhere, but I knew once he arrived and saw all his friends express their love and support for him that he would forgive me with much gratitude.

Debra Young Waller

I went into the other room and got James and
Heather to help me convince Larry to go out the door and
they assisted me in helping him to get into the car safely.

While I was driving Larry to the church, he
expressed his frustration and told me how terrible I was
for being so insensitive to how he was feeling. It took the
Grace of God to hold my peace in a way to not let the cat
out of the bag. I had to 'take it for the team' as they say.
Under my breath I asked the Lord to help me in this
situation, and stay quiet about his birthday surprise.

When we finally arrived to the church under
false pretense of dropping off a USB drive to someone in
the fellowship hall before we go to lunch together, I
prayed Larry wouldn't ask questions about all the cars
parked in the church parking lot.

He assumed it was just another youth fund raiser
they were having at the church. I parked right by the door
of the fellowship hall to make it easier for Larry to go
inside. Now, the next step was to talk Larry out of the car
and get him to walk into the church fellowship hall.
James, my youngest son and Jacob, our oldest walked up
to the car as soon as we pulled up. They helped me
convince their Dad to come in to say hi to the young
people attending the fundraiser before he supposedly was
to go to lunch together afterwards.

Immediately, Larry from a distance down the
foyer of the hall, noticed his best friend, Jack Morgan and
his wife, Paula. As Larry was stunned and trying to

90

process why they were there, over forty-five friends and family who were congregated at the decorated long tables gleefully shouted, "Happy birthday Larry!" My dear sweet husband at that moment, looked down with a humble smile then, softly spoke with a side glance towards me, "I'm sorry". I just simply smiled back at Larry with much love and a tender heart said, "Happy birthday Larry, we all love you; this is your surprise birthday party".

Everybody began singing Happy Birthday in unison. This was a time to celebrate and show Larry how much we all appreciated him. He had given out of himself to so many others throughout the years in full-time ministry. Now these are just a few people who wanted to come together to show their love and appreciation of his friendship that he had always offered to each one of them. Larry always gave a message of hope and peace throughout his walk with the Lord. His sermons were like a sweet fragrance given out like in 2 Corinthians 2:15-16, "For we are the sweet fragrance of Christ [which ascends] to God, [discernible both] among those who are being saved and among those who are perishing. 16) To the latter one an aroma from death to death [a fatal, offensive odor], but to the other an aroma from life to life [a vital fragrance, living and fresh], And who are adequate and sufficiently qualified for these things?" This is what we call the 'Good News of the Gospel'.

Larry reflected the life of a man that had a David's heart. A man who loves his God with all his heart, but also realized that he within himself was imperfect and incomplete without Christ ruling and reigning in his heart. We are saved by Grace not by works lest we should boast, Ephesians 2:8-9. This room full of loved ones was his support group, his cheering crowd who this day indeed encouraged Larry who was celebrating his sixty second birthday. The mission at Larry's birthday party was successful as I stood by and watched those around him shower him with hugs and gifts.

Larry was like a little boy who desperately needed this while each one took pictures with him not knowing this was his last birthday party he would have here on earth. Larry, for a moment in time, gleaned from the harvest of much seed planted from his own efforts of encouraging others. Like seeds planted and watered from his own tears as he prayed for all of them at one time or another, as a friend and an evangelist. This is how ministries are made, shining our light one day at a time.

20

The Week Before Easter, Symptoms of Confusion

It was the week before Easter, a week after we had celebrated Larry's birthday. Spring was in the air and with it a feeling of freshness with a new hope and the renewal of a new day. We were all getting ready to go to church on this Sunday morning. But an unexpected curve in the road left us at another episode of what's next. Larry had a defining moment when he experienced confusion at one of the most simplest tasks, taking a shower. There has been a time when he was disoriented. This diagnosis has been debated on whether the medicine has been causing confusion, or the possibility that the cancer which had been found on the back of Larry's neck in the past had metastasized to his brain.

I noticed that Larry who would routinely take a shower on Sunday mornings had to be reminded this day. When we do life-long routines like daily hygiene we really don't even think about how to accomplish such simple tasks. I had a feeling deep down in myself not to leave Larry alone in the shower this time. As I glanced through the foggy glass shower door, I noticed Larry had a look of, 'How do I start this procedure of putting the soap on the washcloth'. I immediately stepped up to assist Larry to take the simple step by step of taking a shower. As Larry stood in the shower with the body wash in one hand and the washcloth in the other hand, he just stood and kept looking at both hands as if this was the first time in his life that he had done this.

I spoke up at once and requested that he let me assist him. He put his head down with a defeated expression on his face as he replied back to me, "If I can't even remember how to take a shower, how am I going to preach at the upcoming Illinois State Convention?!" I spoke up and said with a sympathetic tone in my voice, "Larry, God will help you, but right now, let me help you take your shower, everything will be okay." I knew in my heart the Lord would not let us down. He had ordered our footsteps for Larry to take a trip in a few weeks to attend the AIGA Illinois State Convention where Larry was scheduled to preach. I then reached in the shower and assisted Larry and I too received a partial shower in the process of helping him.

That afternoon, our grown kids with Jake and Josie's small toddler, Cheyla, came over after church to bring their dad encouragement. I had contacted them and told them why we had not been able to be at church that morning. Since Larry had decided not to go to church that morning, I made him comfortable as he rested in his hospital bed in the middle of our living room. James, our youngest son and his then, girlfriend, Heather, came to the house as well.

Everybody kept the atmosphere as normal as possible with a lively uplifting spirit. I looked over at Larry and witnessed a sad, depressed and defeated expression on his face as he looked down with his eyes glaring in deep thought. Larry had the look of a boxer that just lost a fight. His eyes told the story of what was going on in his head. Years ago, I worked in home-health and heard words of wisdom from one of my dear elderly clients as I took care of her in her home. She had said, "Some people give the devil rent in their head when they need to kick him out."

I, then, got close up to Larry so he would look up at me. With a stern but soft voice I said to him, "Larry, don't give up. Don't give in." He replied back to me, "I can't". I responded again back to him, "Tell me you won't give up now!" Larry, the man of faith had this afternoon put reasoning before truth of "By the stripes of Jesus Christ we are healed." This was the battle he faced today. The devil had whispered in his ear defeat, but I continued to combat these thoughts with words of faith. Larry shot back tenderly, "I can't say that."

I knew the fight was on, I also knew that actions speak louder than words. I turned towards our family who were busy around us preparing lunch and talking with one another, but consciously aware of what was going on at that moment. "Hey you all, come over here by Dad quickly" I urgently said with a nervous tone. They all at once stopped what they were doing and congregated around the hospital bed to get as close as possible to Larry. Josie picked up little Cheyla, our granddaughter so Larry could see her as well.

As I pointed at each one of his family members gathered around him, I said sternly, "Tell your kids you won't give up, they are fighting for you and I'm fighting for you, we won't give up so you can't give up the fight of faith!" Something in Larry just broke as he began to cry. Each one of our adult children with Heather included who had helped me this past few month's care for Larry while I had to work, spoke up.

Their unshakable love and compassion came forth with words of inspiration. This is truly my dream team. This family is and always will be our gift from God. I never felt more proud of each one of them as I did that day when Dad needed them the most. After they gave words of hope like cheerleaders inspiring the team to win, Larry, spoke up again, "If I can't remember, then what's the use for me to go on?"

All of a sudden, the Lord gave me the right answer in the right time, "Larry, the Lord just gave me your answer; remember when you used to have your dually truck that had two gas tanks?" He said, "Yes?" I then continued, "Larry, when one tank went empty of gas, what did you do to keep the truck going?" He thought for a brief moment, and said, "I'd switch on the full tank of gas." That was the answer he needed to hear! I knew the Lord was assisting us with the right words that Larry could relate to. We traveled for many years since our sons had been babies on the road in full-time ministry all across the United States. This was Larry's passion and purpose in life that he could relate to and the Lord knew how to speak his language! I continued, exactly! "Your brain is one tank of gas and your inner man, your spirit is the other tank of gas." I proceeded prompted excitedly by the Holy Spirit, "Now, I'm going to prove this by starting a scripture and you finish it."

Each scripture I started Larry had no trouble remembering the second part of the scripture. He had the word hid in his heart to pull it out like rivers of living water springing up to bring refreshing in the soul. As I continued each line, I pointed at his belly and repeated each time, "Dip the bucket into the well of the spirit". Like David had expressed in the Bible, that he hid the word in his heart that he may not sin against God. "That which is not faith is sin." Romans 14:23.

"But, oh the amazing grace, where sin abounds, grace much more abounds!" Romans 5:20. Once again, the power of darkness and defeat broke. Larry regained his smile as hope rode piggy-backed on faith. His faith once again began to soar. I concluded in this conversation, "Larry, you just dip your bucket into your spirit man when your soul comes up empty. Your spirit is the candle of the Lord. You can do all things through Christ who strengthens you. When you are weak He is strong!" The battle had been won that day as we all sighed with relief.

After that day, Larry had renewed and refreshed his soul with what he always preached, "Hope against hope". Now, he had anticipation in his heart that this is a new day and God is walking with him on this cancer journey while he is declaring his victory. Larry became more than a conqueror through Christ Jesus his Lord.

Easter arrived the following Sunday with the celebration of the resurrection of Jesus Christ. We were back on track, back in church for Easter as a family celebrating our risen King. Afterwards, we all came together enjoying a delicious ham, giving thanks that all was well.

Rev. Larry M Young with wife,
Author Debra Young Waller and family

21

The Dream Foundation; Surprise Visitation of the Lord.

When the battle of life is on, we are to press forward, but through Christ who equips us to succeed no matter what the situation is. God also steps in afterwards to bring us encouragement. Hebrews 4:15 expressed it this way, "For we do not have a High Priest who is unable to understand and sympathize and have a shared feeling with our weaknesses and infirmities and liability to the assaults of temptation, but One who has been tempted in every respect as we are, yet without sinning.

Joshua 1:9, "Have I not commanded you? Be strong and courageous! Do not be terrified or dismayed [intimidated], for the Lord your God is with you wherever you go." God is with us through every situation as he walks with us through the valley of the shadow of death. We don't have to fear evil for He promises that He is with us. Psalms 23:4-5.

When the week had begun with such gloom and defeat, Larry became more than a conqueror, he choose life. Romans 8:37. Easter now was a victory like soldiers regrouping after a bomb hit. The smoke cleared and we again moved forward on this cancer journey.

Debra Young Waller

After Easter, I pondered all the things that had recently happened in our lives. I tried to figure out a way to bring Larry more encouragement to give him inner strength. I wanted to do my part but, I was limited on money. I went before the Lord in prayer again. "Lord, I want to encourage Larry and I know he loves his brothers who live 2,000 miles away in California. They don't have extra money as you know, but I'm asking you to help me fly them here to Missouri to reinforce Larry's strength.

I instantly after praying heard the inner man voice of God speak to my spirit. "Dream Foundation" is what I heard the Lord say to me. Then, God instructed me to type in Google, 'Dream Foundation'. After I typed those two words in, a phone number and information popped up. I didn't even know this Foundation existed. Many years ago when I cared for a client who was going through cancer treatment, while working for Pyramid Home-Health Services, I searched for at least an hour to find a foundation for adults like the Wish Foundation available for children. I then, had absolutely no success.

I clicked on the phone number with great anticipation for the Dream Foundation and the phone began to ring! As I shared our story to the woman on the other line, she listened intently to every detail. This representative for the Dream Foundation guided me to the application site online; I was then, able to print it out. While I was still on the phone with her, she expressed I needed the Hospice nurse, Jennifer, to help me fill out the application. Jennifer and I both did our part and I mailed in the application to the Dream Foundation on a Thursday morning.

To my amazement, the following Monday, the Dream Foundation contacted me. Larry's application for the Dream Foundation was approved! I cried, laughed and jumped up and down with such joy and happiness! This was truly another great miracle in the making.

Larry's desire was to have his brothers both fly out and all expenses paid. Not only did the Dream Foundation fly out both brothers, but they paid for airfare, motel, rental car and extra money for food to go out to eat with the family. Praise the Lord! With God *all* things are possible. Matthew 19:26.

Within the next three days since the phone call, the Dream Foundation contacted both of Larry's brothers. Larry was overwhelmed with joy. He knew and experienced the Glory of God. The Word was confirmed with signs and wonders as the Lord was working with us. Mark 16:20. They were to be flown out in three days! The arrival time would be by Thursday afternoon.

I contacted our grown children and my best friend, Judy about this whole even that would be taking place by the Dream Foundation but orchestrated only by God in just three days. Then, I contacted Larry's other best friend, Wesley Waller, to join us in this special event.

Each one of us acted like a team to do what we could to make this adventurous miracle a success. God had Larry's back through every second of the 3-4 day visit. The Dream foundation had offered for the Brothers to stay a little longer but, one of the brothers had to get back to work at his California residence.

The Great I Am held Larry's hand and didn't relax his hold on him. Hebrews 13:5. God held Larry's hand while he walked through the fire alongside the cancer journey in his life. This is something in life not many get to experience, divine appointment set up by God. This book now, because of our written testimony of this great event, is exposed to you, the reader.

As Larry and I came to the garden of God, never letting go of the one we knew with all our heart loves us, God came to us with a visitation of His glory. There is an example of those who did not recognize the time of God's visitation in Luke 19:42-44. "If you had known on this day, [of salvation, even you, the things which make for peace [and on which peace depends] But now they have been hidden from your eyes. 43) For a time [of siege] is coming when your enemies will put up a barricade [with pointed stakes] against you, and surround you [with armies] and hem you in on every side. 44) And they will level you to the ground, you [Jerusalem] and your children within you. They will not leave in you one stone on another, all because you did not come progressively to] recognize [from observation and personal experience] the time of your visitation {when God was gracious toward you and offered you salvation]."

What if we had become weary in well doing from not staying connected to the vine of God's presence? When life hits a person hard with unexpected circumstances, this is the time we have to press on even harder to not let go. This is the 'fight of faith' in action. When we are weak He is strong. At the same time, we are trophies displayed by God to bring encouragement to others so that they can say, 'If God can do this for them, He can do this for me!' Oh, but how the Lord desires to bless us in every part of our lives.

The Lord desires to bring rays of sunshine to each one of us on our journey of life. Great men that have gone on before us have experienced the glory of God when they made a choice to believe that He is and He is a rewarder to those who diligently seek him. Hebrews 11:6. God wants to reveal Himself to us more than we want him to. He said He will never leave us nor forsake us. Hebrews 13:5. God is the same yesterday, today and forever, Hebrews 13:8.

During those few days, we all laughed, cried, hugged and shared stories of the past. Each one of us gently and respectfully took turns sitting next to Larry at home as he sat up in his hospital bed. Every moment was strategically set in order by God. No man could have planned this special event so well. These were memories we now treasure for the rest of our lives as family and close friends. Not one moment was wasted as we held Larry up in honor and love.

After those days were done, and Larry's brothers flew back home we, as a family, reflected back to what had just took place. We were all equipped by God to be encouraged to go forward, one step at a time on this cancer journey.

Rev. Larry M Young with his brothers.

22

The Last Road Trip as an Evangelist, the Illinois State Convention

God had opened up an opportunity a few months before for Larry to preach at the AIGA Illinois State Convention. He had not, at that time, when he accepted this invitation to speak had memory struggles. Larry was challenged recently with not only weakness and pain, but also gathering his thoughts to do even simple tasks.

I had noticed Larry struggling when I would hand him his Bible which he had studied for many years. He couldn't comprehend what he tried to read. He looked at the scripture in the Bible with a blank look on his face as he tried to read what was in front of him. I reached for Larry's hand and prayed with him for healing of the mind. Larry was always prepared with notes for every sermon as he studied intensely to be prepared to speak. This time, his memory was blocked as if the brain had short-circuited. His ability to comprehend even the simplest words were blocked.

The Illinois State convention was just a few days away and we had to come up with some type of preparation to this dilemma. The messages in the past always came from the Lord even though Larry made much preparation through prayer and study. I prayed fervently for Larry with him in agreement, "Lord, show us what you want Larry to share in your word and open up his heart and mind to receive."

By faith, I went into Larry's office where he kept his past sermons in his file cabinet and desk. In desperation, I went through the messages and picked out a few typed up sermons. I knew even with these typed scriptures and notes, God would give Larry a new perspective as the *rhema* of the word would come alive in his spirit. Then, as if my mind targeted in on a particular page, I felt I was being led by faith to the right sermon.

The year before, Larry had held a class called, 'Healing School' where he taught in the church on a Saturday morning the concept of healing to help others to achieve answers to their prayers through the understanding of the scriptures which dealt with healing. These classes unfolded what prayer is all about and the emphasis of the power of prayer. He broke down the scriptures in the Greek and the Hebrew meaning.

I then brought these papers to Larry who was resting on his bed waiting for an answer to this problem of preparing for the Illinois State Convention meeting. I sat next to Larry and proceeded to read his own typed notes as he listened intently. We both knew after the great event from the Dream Foundation the past week, that God had this and He would not let us down.

All of the sudden, I heard in my heart to ask Larry if he and Jack Morgan, his other best friend could do a double-header sermon. You see, a double-header sermon is when there are two speakers who work together sharing the platform and preaching the sermon together as a team. One speaker begins the sermon and the other speaker takes the second half of the sermon. Larry had done this type of preaching in the past and immensely enjoyed this type of service, especially with his best friend, Jack Morgan. Larry lit up with excitement and agreed to do this.

Now, the next day, I called the Illinois State Committee Chairman, and their Committee Board decided that this was a good idea. I called Jack Morgan and filled him in on the medical issues Larry was having. I asked him if he could help Larry by Larry's request and approval as well. Jack was more than happy to help his best friend and brother in this way. Now, the plan would be set with approval from all. Little did Jack know this would be his last opportunity to preach with his long-time friend.

The day finally came to prepare Larry to go on this long trip. Judy, our close friend, was to be the driver for us to get there along with Jake, Josie and our little granddaughter, Cheyla. We had a motel room waiting for us when we would arrive. Our caravan of two vehicles was prepared to take on this challenge. We'd already seen what God had just done as a family and knew he would carry out his perfect plan. James, our youngest son and Heather, his now, Fiancé, did their part by helping Larry get dressed for the special occasion.

Debra Young Waller

We arrived at the motel and got everything
unloaded. Larry had just enough time before the service
to rest and recuperate from the long trip. Then it was time
to go to the church for the meeting in Grafton, Illinois.
The meeting had just started when we all arrived at the
church. Jake, Judy and Josie along with myself, helped
Larry get out of the vehicle and into the building with his
walker holding him up. As we were walking up to the
door, I could hear the congregation singing praise and
worship.

As the service proceeded to the next part of the
program, Larry was called up to the front. We sat on the
front row so Larry wouldn't have too much struggle
walking up there with his walker. After he sat on a chair
they prepared for him, he requested for me to sing, "I
claim the Blood". While I was singing, I looked forward
from the pulpit at Larry as he sat in the chair facing the
congregation, worshiping his Lord and Savior. Only God
knows what he was thinking or praying while I was
singing my song.

After I sang, I stepped down to the seat at the
front row anticipating what would God do now? Larry's
notes were in front of him with his Bible as he sat there,
with a pause as if he was waiting on the Lord to show him
what to do. He closed his eyes as he bowed down his
head in prayer.   Then suddenly, he grasped hold of his
walker in front of him and instantly stood up with the
strength of the Lord. Larry began to speak with a soft
spoken voice, but with confidence as faith was released
like a faucet being turned on. The rivers of living water

108

began to flow from within His spirit man as God was lighting a candle that began to blaze with the fire of the Holy Ghost.

I glanced down at his notes that were in front of him and noticed he had not used even one line that was typed on the page. As he continued to speak, the scriptures came out of his mouth with authority and power as the word came alive to offer strength to not only him in his own convictions, but also all those who that day witnessed another miracle of God's power and strength in that little church this day. Later on, I found out someone had recorded the whole sermon on their cell phone. God is so good!

I watched with such bewilderment, knowing the battle we'd had only a few days before and not knowing how God was going to do this. As I looked at Larry, who appeared to be this fragile man, open his mouth I witnessed as the Lord filled it with the message that came from the throne of God. Only God had the answer and He chose to use Larry for His Glory. Larry spoke for at least 25 minutes while he received the echoes from the congregation responding with shouts of 'Amen' and 'Hallelujah'. After Larry finished what the Lord gave him, he graciously handed the service over to his best friend, Jack Morgan, to take the other half of the sermon. Jack flowed eloquently as the message carried the weight of power. Larry and Jack that afternoon became the dynamic duo, a team with God Almighty as others witnessed the greatness of God's anointing in action.

After the service had ended, they were having a luncheon. The members prepared Larry and I a plate to eat upstairs so Larry wouldn't have to walk downstairs to the fellowship hall. While we were sitting in our chairs they provided for us at the back of the auditorium, Larry became overwhelmed with fatigue, he was, at this point, wiped out. He expressed he had to go back to the motel room and lay down. Judy, along with me and our family helped him to get back in the car and left the church to go back to the motel. Larry crashed on the bed and slept all afternoon. Then, in the late night, he woke up not knowing where he was or who we were. Jennifer, his hospice nurse, had sent his medication with us which helped him calm down. She gave us instructions to help him if this did occur while we were away on this trip.

The next morning, we prepared to leave and go home. We had a great victory even though afterwards the medical condition overwhelmed his body and mind. These events displayed that after we come before the Lord in prayer, He takes the wheel and does what we can't do.

After we got Larry home, he rested in his hospital bed, knowing again, God continued to walk with him when he stepped out in faith.

Rev. Larry M Young
Preaching at the Illinois State A.I.G.A. Convention.

Success comes from never giving up, never giving in. We should never quit right before the manifestation God already has prepared for those who believe. Failure is throwing in the towel before experiencing the miracles in our lives whether big or small, our lives should glorify God so that one day he will say, "Well done my good and faithful servant" Matthew 25:21. As we do our very best to walk by faith and not by sight we learn, "Man plans his way but God directs his steps", Proverbs 16:9.

23

An Unexpected Blessing; Help is on the Way

I noticed, at this stage of the cancer journey, that Larry's overall medical condition was declining. We continued to, consistently as before, listen to television Preachers teach and preach the word of faith. Larry also listened to praise and worship with his CD player. His memory and reasoning difficulties had become more evident now. Larry's nurse, Jennifer, suspected this could be a combination of fatigue and possibly the cancer on the neck had indeed metastasized to his brain.

My biggest concern now, was how do I continue working full-time and be there to help care for Larry in his condition. I have to continue to work to pay the bills and buy food. If I took off work that would mean less money for all the co-payments as well. I always known that God is my provider, but I've always tried to reason and plan a strategy.

Larry had been forgetting proper words to use in simple sentences. Often, Larry would forget where he was and who certain people were who were close to him. The most devastating times were without notice, his brain would kick into what they call, 'fight or flight' mode. The panic would set in as he became intolerably defensive creating a situation in his mind of suspicion to those around him as if his family had wrong motives and wrong intentions. This type of behavior was completely impulsive and followed up with a spaced-out look in his eyes. It was if a light bulb was turned off or sometimes like a flickering light was about to burn out.

One day, when I was at work, Heather called me in a panic while she stayed with Larry as his care-giver during the day. I had only been at work for just a few hours when the phone rang.

Larry had wandered impulsively out the front door, stepped down the step as if he was trying to escape thinking he was kidnapped. He tripped and fell in a roll drop into the grass. We only unlock the front door during the day because of the fight or flight episodes to let the Hospice nurse and I come in. Usually this happened in the middle of the night mimicking Sundowners.

Thank goodness Heather had her cell phone right with her for emergency situations. I quickly left work and drove home as fast as I could. While I had Heather on the phone, I instructed her to sing a gospel song to him to calm him down and pray softly for him as he sat on the grass determined not to get up even with assistance. His brain somehow had short-circuited.

I was almost home, still on the phone with Heather when I requested that she put the phone where Larry could hear my voice. I spoke to him calmly, "Larry, this is Deb, your wife and I'm on my way home to see you". Surprisingly, he shot back with a sarcastic tone,

"You're lying, you aren't Debbie, you're trying to fool me," I then mentioned the pet name he had given me twenty-six years ago and used frequently. He said, "Someone told you that to trick me!" It was hard to comprehend that this was my husband whom I've been married to for over twenty-six years. I had to pray for the Lord to give me strength and courage as well as wisdom to what I should do after I pull up in the driveway and get out of my car.

When I pulled up in the driveway and got out of my car, I saw Larry sitting on the grass and looking down in much confusion. I pretended I was coming home for Lunch and wanted to join him. Softly I spoke, "Larry, let's go inside and have lunch, I don't want to eat on the grass today." "Look around you. Now, let's go on and get up and eat lunch together." Thank goodness Larry agreed after he gave the idea much thought. Heather and I then before he could change his mind, helped him get up and in the house.

Needless to say, I stayed home for the rest of the day. I immediately called Jennifer, Larry's nurse and briefed her about the episode that had just taken place. She came as soon as she could and took hold of the situation with skill and compassion. This type of trauma wasn't like anything I'd ever seen or experienced before. Lord, I prayed, help me deal this this emotional roller coaster as we claim Larry's healing. I knew we had just witnessed a new stage in the cancer journey, but also knew the Lord would guide us through with His amazing grace.

Debra Young Waller

Every morning I escaped to my prayer closet, the bathroom, and I would cry out to God on my knees as I touched heaven on Larry's behalf and for strength for me and my family. I continued to miss more work and had to at the same time trust the Lord to provide for our needs.

Judy, our best friend who was with us on this journey every step of the way, offered an ear to listen. I confided in Judy and knew she would pray with me for a solution to this situation we were facing financially.

A few days later, Joan, our Church missionary director from The Rose of Sharon Full Gospel Temple in DeSoto, Missouri contacted me. This is one of those times when an unexpected answer to prayer came. They as part of the missions department, offered to reimburse me for the time I had to miss from work to care for Larry. For many years Larry preached encouraging messages and we had helped at Christmas time with the food boxes and gift bags of toys, but now, the church had reached out to us when we needed them the most.

Praise the Lord! The heavy burden had lifted when someone answered the call, to come my way after I have prayed! God had reached out to someone's heart and they had answered the call.

24

The Last Benefit Singing, Bitter-Sweet End

Our dear friend, Carrie, a servant of the Lord, orchestrated a Gospel Singing to help raise money for the bills and co-payments to sustain us for the next few months. We were so very grateful to know there were so many true Christians in this world who choose to be a blessing as they reached out to us in our darkest hour.

As each day came closer to the big event, I found out the gospel groups who would participate were Heartfelt, the Tindall Family and friends. The Redemptions had previously volunteered as well. When Larry was coherent in his thoughts, I shared the information with him. He was overjoyed with enthusiasm knowing there are those who cared as they did their part to be a blessing to our family.

The gospel singing was a success with joy and tears of gratitude. Larry sat in his wheel chair during the singing with his arm raised, praising the Lord. I saw a glimpse of peace on his face as I sat next to him, holding his other hand in mine. As the service was coming to a close, the speaker requested for all to stand and praise the Lord. No one expected Larry to stand from his wheel chair, but without hesitation he stood as he shook to steady himself. He was weak, but wanted to give honor to his God. Heather and Jacob stood nearby and saw Him struggle to stand. They immediately went to Larry and helped him sit back down in his wheelchair. Larry gleamed wide-eyed and had a big smile on his face with satisfaction that this has been a great night.

It was time to leave, but Larry didn't want to go home. I knew it was extremely necessary for him to take his medications which were slightly past due at this time. I then talked to my son to go get the car and pull it to the front door of the church. Right before we went out the door, there was someone who wanted to take our picture as a family hovered around Larry and his wheel chair. I will always treasure this picture because it was the last one we had with the whole family together.

It was a struggle trying to get Larry into the car. It appeared that he was becoming confused again. We knew we had to get him home as soon as possible. His eyes looked glazed over as if he was slipping into a trance. James and Heather were driving close behind me. As I pulled into the driveway with just me and Larry in the car, Larry suddenly looked over at me with wide eyes and had the expression of panic and fear. With an anxious tone he said, "Who are you lady?" Who are you driving my car!" He repeated this phrase several times. I was taken by surprise at this wondering what to do next. "Lord, help me please", I cried under my breath.

My words were few but tender, I spoke up, "I'm your wife, Larry, and this is my car I brought you home in; We just came back home from the gospel singing". He argued back, "You kidnapped me, I don't know who you are, let me go right now". I proceeded to lock the door so he wouldn't fall out of the car in the dark driveway.

As I scrambled to get my cell phone out and call Jake and Josie to come immediately, they had just stopped at a gas station before going back home from the church. At that moment, Larry figured out how to unlock the car door and began trying to open the door while exclaiming, "I'm calling the police, let me go now!" I held the phone with my left hand as I grabbed Larry with my right hand and begged him not to leave the car. James called me that second to let me know he was close to the house now. The tension continued to rise when; it began out of nowhere to rain in the dark.

Larry continued to struggle, but was still too weak to push out the door to get away from this strange women who he didn't recognize, sitting next to him in the driver's seat. Suddenly, thunder boomed in the air with a flash of lightening. This storm seemed to make the matter much worse. As the storm intensified so did the drama in the driveway. Larry continued yelling, "She robbed a bank and is kidnapping me. Help, help!" Our grown kids rushed up to the car at that moment and took charge as Larry said, "Get that woman away from me. Get her away from me!"

I at this point was broken as I cried out within my very being, "Lord help me, help Larry, help me get him in the house". I knew I had to get out of the car since I seemed to be the panic button in Larry's mind, but right now I had to keep him right here with me until help arrived. James and Heather pulled up at this time and took over and I went in the house shaking as I held back the tears to stay strong from not understanding but comprehending he had symptoms of an alzheimer's patient. Larry somehow had gotten into the driver's seat and Heather stayed right by him. He turned to Heather and urgently said, "We have to get the car keys and get out of here, go get the car keys." Heather though, hurried to the door and asked for Larry's medicine that calmed him down prescribed by the Hospice nurse, Jennifer. All four of our kids, Jake, James, Josie and Heather were at the car door trying to persuade Larry to come inside the house while Jacob assisted in giving Larry the medicine. Finally, with the down-pouring rain, they decided to physically lift Larry out of the car and sit him in the wheel chair. They then proceeded to carry Larry with the Wheelchair to the front door and help him in the house.

Each one of them was drenched from the downpour along with Larry who was soaked. As the two women helped Larry to undress and take off the wet clothes, I grabbed towels and dry clothes to change him while he struggled to get free from them who were assisting him.

All of a sudden, Josie, our daughter in law began singing his favorite song, "In the Garden". Each one of us joined in unison. You could feel the tangible presence of the Lord as Larry began joining in with us. There's something special about the anointing that sets the captive free. Larry calmed down and came to his senses. The power of God reconnected the short-circuits in his brain. When he was responding with alzheimer symptoms, he was not in pain and had much strength. But, when he came back to his senses, it was as if the brain re-connected not only his reasoning, but also the nerves that sent pain throughout his body.

The Lord fought this battle with us when we knew not what to do. My emotions were soaring like a roller coaster as I fought the good fight of faith, not only for Larry's sake, but also my own. Those thoughts of why did this even have to happen to our family who continued to serve the Lord. But as I have heard a minister say, "I don't just have faith in getting what I've asked, but for a higher purpose. I have faith in trusting that God has a perfect plan to reach many souls for His Glory." I just want to do this life right. We have only one chance to make it count and now it's our turn to give our lives away to demonstrate how to trust the Lord even when we don't understand.

I can't even put into words how proud and thankful I am for our Young family who, when they stood in the fire of life, their faith in God was stronger than their pain. They came together that night with Godly character while they showed the fruits of the spirit and worked together in unity. A three chord rope that is tightly wound cannot be broken when God is allowed to take charge. It is a choice we all have to make.

The Lord worked with each one, doing their part as each one that night became the heroes while only recognizing the need to reach out to their Dad. They shared his burden and grief following the instructions of the Holy Spirit.

The next day, my cousin, Sandra Weber, her husband Kenny and my uncle Carl McKalip, who is also my Pastor, paid us a visit. They sat down next to Larry's bed facing me as I sat on the other side of the hospital bed, I was choked up as I tried to share to them what had happened after the Gospel fundraiser singing. They all three listened intensely as my eyes welled up with tears feeling like I lost my best friend to this brain malfunction. Sandy spoke up with words of compassion, "Did you know when those who go through this and turn on you as if you were a stranger, those are the loved ones that are the closest to them who they turn on the most." When she shared that information, all of a sudden, I felt a distorted sort of comfort knowing, well I must be that much more special to my Larry. Who would have ever known when faced with such complexity of the mind. The brain had a way of turning his thoughts upside down like a coin being flipped around, heads or tails, not knowing where it would land.

25

Words of Gratitude From My Husband, Larry

There were good days where I treasured just a glimpse of normality in Larry's eyes, the days when he wasn't spaced out. It felt like when you put a piece of chocolate in your mouth and savor the flavor to make it last longer. Larry got that twinkle in his eye and spoke to me with such love and appreciation this day as he expressed how much he was thankful and appreciated all I had done for him this past few years. When the Hospice team came in, he never missed a chance to express his gratitude to them as well.

Debra Young Waller

26

When Little Things Mean a Lot

Our dear church family, a retired couple, Carolyn and Tom were coming to the house often and offered their help with little things around the house while paying Larry a visit to cheer him up and speak words of faith to encourage him. Larry would light up with a smile as he always looked forward to their visits.

My cousin, Shannon also came to visit to share scriptures and words of faith in the promises of God to Larry. After Shannon left, the whole atmosphere would change. You could feel the faith rise in all of us. The effect of her uplifting words was like a sweet fragrance that filled the air. Several others would also pay Larry a visit to bring encouragement.

Little do we realize how important the simple things are to reach out to those who are facing hardships. These are simple acts of kindness expressed as showing the love of God in a practical way. In Matthew 25:35, "For I was hungered and ye gave me meat: I was thirst, and ye gave me drink; I was a stranger, and ye took me in, 36) Naked and ye clothed me: I was sick, and ye visited me: I was in prison, and ye came to me. Farther down these scriptures the Lord added, "40) And the king shall answer and say unto them, Verily I say unto you,

Inasmuch as ye have done it unto one of the least of these my brethren, ye have done it unto me.

These are unsung heroes in our lives, never praising their own works but giving Glory to God. One day they will hear, "Well done my good and faithful Servant." Matthew 25:21.

27

The Roller Coaster

The ups and downs were very unpredictable day by day. We were extremely grateful for the good days, but each day we noticed Larry slipping through our fingers. At times, especially in the middle of the night, while James slept on the couch right by his Dad's hospital bed in the living room, Heather in the guest room and I in my bed with the door open where I could see every move Larry made, Larry would forget who he was and forget who we were. He wandered out of bed like a lost boy who was confused as to where he was. I kept the walker right next to Larry's bed just in case he would space out and try to walk because he was weak and unsteady with each step. We also, had to put a chain lock at the top of the door so he wouldn't get out the door and fall in the night before we could reach him. We had very little sleep, but we knew that we had to be alert at all times.

We were constantly checking Larry's vitals, but as Larry progressed in his symptoms, I realized he wasn't eating like he had been before. I prayed again with this problem of him not wanting to eat. Then, all of a sudden, God gave me a recipe for healthy muffins that had all the nutrition his body would need and they tasted good to Larry. I called them pumpkin muffins made with coconut flour and almond flour. All ingredients were healthy and sweetened with honey and stevia. Larry simply loved these muffins and ate them throughout the day.

28

The Visit to Heaven

Heather and the Hospice team took care of Larry during the day, and Heather, James and I cared for Larry in the evening. James and I would stay up most of the night caring for Larry, because if he was awoken he would be in a fight-or-flight state of mind. James would sleep on the couch and I slept in the bedroom, just a few feet away, with the door open. We were all Larry's caregivers, sharing in responsibility willingly with our heart to assist him however we could, with each one of us doing our part.

Larry, more frequently now, had to be protected from his own mind and reasoning like an alzheimer patient whose reality is distorted while the memory of close loved ones fade. The brain cells continued to short-circuit from the damage done when the cancer metastasized to the brain. I was extremely impressed of how the hospice team took care of him.

Jennifer kept a close eye on Larry's medication and adjusted it frequently to a perfect balance to meet the demand of the symptoms. Words of encouragement to our family were given by the Hospice team with a light heart to help all of us who cared for him.

One morning I was startled from my sleep by the sound of Larry crying hysterically. I immediately ran to sit next to him on his bed. Not knowing what was going on, I asked sympathetically, "Larry, what's wrong, are you okay?" He replied with tears flowing down his face and a glazed look in his eyes, as if he had just been given bad news, "I saw him! I had to go back; he said I had to go back!" He sobbed. "He told me he's not done with me yet."

My mind at this point tried to sort all of this information out. Then, it occurred to me, Larry was saying he died and the Lord told him to come back because it was not his time. I then, spoke up, "Larry, did you go to Heaven last night and see Jesus?" He confirmed, "Yes." I was relieved thinking, okay, he's going to be with us longer because God has work for him to do. That means manifestation of a miracle! I spoke up with a smile of relief on my face, "Oh good Larry, he sent you back to me. That's good!" He then quickly said, "No!" But with my surprise Larry answered again, "No!"

I knew deep inside my heart the pain and struggle with his memory coming and going had taken its toll on my dear sweet husband. He has fought this fight of faith for almost four years now and was getting weary. How can I compete with Heaven! Now, Larry had gotten a glimpse of Heaven and possibly those who had gone on before him. Most of all, he got a glimpse of the Lord, Jesus Christ his Savior who had walked with him throughout this whole cancer journey.

Miracles on the Cancer Journey

Though Larry's spirit man knew well God's promises of healing are true, the suffering and the confusion episodes were, I believed, affecting his emotions and reasoning to think clearly right now. He had always spoke faith and never wavered until the memory began to alter his brain.

As Larry's wife and help-mate, I mustered encouragement with a desperate but loving tone, the spoken words of faith and hope, "Larry, you have such a testimony to carry around the world of the faithfulness of God and his healing power to all. Don't give up, Larry, don't give in now. You are on the verge of your miracle at the midnight hour!"

That day, we continued caring for Larry as if nothing happened with his normal routine. The CD player continued to play softly all Larry's favorite praise and worship songs, mostly songs sung by the Tindall Family and Friends gospel group. His favorite faith preachers continued at the best selected times of day as well.

A few more days had passed since Larry had his encounter of a glimpse of Heaven. I could sense a decline in him physically and well as his emotions. He now was more solemn as he laid on the hospital bed resting more often with his eyes closed. His appetite also declined has he no longer desired to eat. I could feel him slipping through my fingers as the nurse explained to me what exactly was happening when a patient was dying. Still, I believed that with God all things were possible. I will not give up but, I knew I had to hold tight when he couldn't.

Larry had for so many years since the beginning of our marriage, been my Prince Charming. This past few months when there were moments I didn't recognize who he was, I knew he was still with me, the man I fell in love with. I again, slipped to the bathroom and knelt before my Lord as I cried out, "Lord, I know with you all things are possible, I need your strength and Grace, and Larry needs your glory of a miracle." As the tears rolled down my cheeks and my face bowed before my Lord, I began feeling his anointing cover me with a peace that passes all understanding. All is well, all is well with my soul.

29

The Plea

I was awoken at the break of dawn with another sound from Larry's bed as he pleaded to God, "Take me home Lord, please, take me home. Unless you heal this body, take me home." My heart sunk deep in my soul, but I was led of the Lord, do not interfere this time. So, I recorded this plea with my cell phone behind the doorway as I looked up to heaven crying in disappointment.

Is he praying out of his head or is this a sincere real heart plea unto the Lord? It was so hard to tell the difference now. Only God knew because he knew how to communicate with Larry's spirit who was healed and whole. Then, finally I got the release to stop the recording and step into the room to sit by Larry on his bed. No one can truly understand the battles we fight until they have walked in another's shoes.

This true warrior has fought courageously many battles in life and always was my encourager. He was walking through the valley of the shadow of death, but knew the Lord continued to hold his hand. I didn't leave the house now, but stayed close to my dear husband, Larry.

Debra Young Waller

30

The Birthday Party

The Thursday before Larry took his last breath, it was June 8, 2017. Our oldest Son, Jacob had his birthday, so we all came together at my house to celebrate with his Dad, Larry. After I had heard Larry the week before pray for the Lord to take him home, I prayed by myself in the bathroom, on my knees, touching Heaven. "Lord, I come again in your presence with another request; I believe you are able to turn this all around for your Glory. I also know our times are in your hand. Please Lord, let Larry live to be with his family and loved ones for Jacob's birthday celebration and be in his right mind." I still claimed a manifestation of healing whether raised from the dead or instant miracle.

We celebrated that special day with Judy and Wes around Larry's hospital bed. Everybody was smiling and rejoicing together while Larry was at peace among us. The Lord had answered our prayers. Though Larry had seemed very solemn and didn't say much of anything, but stayed quiet. When Wes had gotten up to leave, he touched Larry who was lying still in his hospital bed in the living room. All of a sudden, Larry woke up, and recognized Wes' touch on his shoulder. We couldn't understand what Larry said except his name, but the enthusiasm in his voice was cheery and responsive. We may never understand the concept of this response, but we were all glad Larry half raised and lit up.

Later that day, I escaped alone, on my knees and thanked my Lord for such a special memory that God had created that day with the family and with those who were very close to us all.

All of us had not mentioned to each other why these things had to take place when all of us believed then and still believe now that the word is true and does not return void. We choose instead not to lean on our own understanding, but acknowledge Him in all our ways while the Lord was directing our path. Proverbs 3:5-6.

31

Raised From the Dead

As Friday approached, Larry was using what I called, 'the breathing machine'. We continued throughout the day checking his oxygen capacity and oxygen levels while staying close by his bed.

I could feel my sweet Larry slipping through my fingers. Those who were there were all our grown children, our best friend Judy and Katie, her daughter who was also my spiritual, adopted daughter.

All of us tried to act as normal as possible through the day and night as Jake, Josie, Heather, James and Katie played monopoly at the kitchen table which was an open floor plan close by their Dad. Judy and I sat around Larry in his hospital bed in the living room engaged in small talk.

Larry laid there motionless and unresponsive during this time. The oxygen tank as the late night approached, gradually had to be raised continuously to assist Larry's breathing. I still, even at this point, believed that any moment the manifestation of his miracle would take place.

Each one of us took turns sitting or standing next to Larry in the middle of the night and shared encouraging words and spoken personal communication to him. We waited not knowing what else to do, but as the word says in Ephesians 6:13, "and having done everything [that the crisis demands,] to stand firm in your place, fully prepared, immovable, victorious.

I was so very tired by now, but I knew I must stay alert and ready for anything. When I looked at the clock, it was in the middle of the night. The oxygen was as high as it was able to be set. There was absolutely nothing else we could do, but to be there for Larry and be in continued prayer for him. I fought with everything in my being, now the rest was up to the Lord.

The many thoughts flooded my mind, 'What else could I have done to be a good help-mate for him. Did I do everything in my power? Could I have said more to build up his faith? Was Larry hungry and could he feel pain lying there in his bed?' I felt so powerless now, only able to sit there and wait. I know God heard my thoughts from a far off. Psalms 139:2. As I continued to pray, "Lord, at what point will your glory be manifested here on earth today, for such a time as this?" The Great I AM was silent was we waited.

In my mind I, deeply in thought wondered, is Larry right now, in his right mind and coherent or does he understand who he is or who we were around him? Jennifer, the Hospice nurse had just a few days ago, showed us with a small light, he was going blind as his eyes did not respond to the flash of the light.

The time continued to slip away as I looked at the clock once more and It showed after 3:30 a.m. Saturday morning. Larry was slightly struggling to breathe, but there was nothing we could do about it. Katie stood next to her spiritual Dad as we sat close by and said, *"He's gone"*. Larry, the Great Man of God had passed away.

I immediately walked around to the side of the bed next to Katie with my heart torn apart and completely broken within me full of disappointment and grief. There just isn't enough words to describe this moment in time. We were all standing together around the bed in much grief.

Suddenly the presence of God overwhelmed me with His amazing grace. The Anointing saturated my very being with courage and strength that could only come from God. A supernatural feeling of power and authority stepped in like the batter stepping up at the plate to hit a home run.

Without any hesitation, I burst out loud, with my finger pointing at Larry next to him, I demanded, "Larry, in the name of Jesus, I command you to come back now; I command you to live!"

Suddenly, Larry gasped for air as if he was coming out of water! He opened his eyes and looked up at me in much surprise. He was communicating with me with his baby blue eyes, just staring back at me and breathing hard.

I then continued to speak to him while my heart yearned for his response to continue to live, "Larry, I respect your choice and God's choice for you, but I do not want to let go of you! I love you Larry, I don't want to let you go, but I'll respect your choice right now."

We began to sing "How Great Thou Art". As we continued to sing, Larry began breathing more calmly and closed his eyes as his breathing became more shallow and faint. We sung with our hearts focused on the Lord and His amazing grace and love towards all of us.

All of a sudden, as we continued singing as we worshiped our God, we could feel the room fill up with Heaven's glory as Larry was drifting away unto death. He had made his choice. I don't know if I can really call this death at this moment or passing on to the other side.

It felt like Larry was being ushered home into another realm of his life, he was going home. This was a gentle sweep of the amazing grace of God, so gently releasing Larry from all the pain and suffering he endured here on earth. Larry fought a good fight and kept the faith for almost four years here on the cancer journey. He proclaimed the promises of God, unwavering as he preached and taught to others during this time on earth, how to persevere through contradicting circumstances while his body endured such great suffering and pain.

Miracles on the Cancer Journey

We all felt the presence of the Lord greater than any miracle we had ever witnessed in our entire lives that early morning, June 10. 2017. Nobody could deny that we had a visitation from God. Larry was, that day, born in heaven rejoicing with those who had gone on before him. He had accomplished his purpose here on earth and finished his course just like the word says in 2 Timothy 4:7-8.

My phone buzzed with a notification from somebody at that very moment at 4:05 a.m. after Larry took his last and final breath. Judy brought this to my attention as we both were very surprised. A great prayer warrior, Charlene, who lived far from us had sent a message on Messenger. She said, "I just had a vision of him entering Heaven. It was quite a fanfare, I love you my dear sister. There was such joy on his face."

I responded back to Charlene, "Wowie confirmation. I'm broken, thank you." Then her replied back was, "I'm praying for you and will continue to do so. Love you so much, Mighty Woman of God." After that, Charlene said she knew she felt the Holy Spirit then, God gave her this vision. It seems by my own experiences, the hotter the fire, the greater the glory of God will be manifested in our lives. You never know how nor when God will reveal Himself in your journey called life.

Debra Young Waller

32

Reflecting on the Miracles; Life and Death

Larry was always my Elijah, as I have been with him in ministry for over seventeen years, traveling and spreading the good news of the Gospel of Jesus Christ. In the beginning I was so very shy and unsure of myself, just as Elisha was in the beginning of his journey with Elijah.

Now, my mentor and husband had passed on to the other side as I sat down and reflected on what had just taken place. Another soldier had gone home. He fought a good fight and kept the faith; Larry was accepting his rewards in the presence of the Lord. "What do I do now?" Was in my thoughts as I cried with tears streaming down my face. I heard a voice in my spirit say," Now, it's your turn to go forward as a Warrior for Christ as you finish your course on your journey." "It's time to go to the next level of My glory."

I can't look back except to reflect on what the Lord has done on this cancer journey which came to an end, or so I thought, to give him praise with my life now.

I choose to take those things I have learned and experienced as a witness for the Lord to reach out to others and make a difference in their lives. God had just raised the dead just like he instructed us in Matthew 10:8, "Heal the sick, raise the dead, cleanse those who have

143

leprosy, drive out demons, freely you have received; freely give.

Recently, I reflected back to when Larry told me as he laid in his hospital bed one morning, he saw the Lord, but he told him to go back. Larry had seen the Lord and after seeing Heaven and Christ in all of His glory, he didn't want to come back. He said," I have seen him, I was with him." How could anybody compete with that, I can only imagine.

Did Larry see our children and grandchildren that brief moment in Heaven? I almost envied him to witness such grandeur.

33

It's My Turn Now, To Give My Life Away

Now, I'm on a path to find out who I am in Christ and Him crucified. I Corinthians 2:2-5. My next great adventure as I continued to type in my journal since January, 2017, around five months before Larry passed on, is to be without him.

I have to find out where do I go from here. There's only one thing to do and that is take one day at a time and make the most of every opportunity as I acknowledge the Lord in all my ways and he will direct my path, Proverbs 3:5-6. This is new beginnings; a new chapter has begun in all of our lives while we encourage one another in the faith.

God, as a skillful writer, holds the pen and writes in my book all the days of my life. Each chapter of all of our lives is carefully written with His plans and purposes as He receives the glory. As I read in Psalms 139, I hear how David explained it all so well. This life is to be continued until the coming of the Lord.

Debra Young Waller

34

In Memory of Rev. Larry M. Young

This book is dedicated in memory of my Late Husband, Reverend Larry Morton Young.

He left quite a legacy which has and will change the future of all who reads this book. Larry dedicated his life and his death to represent what faith is all about.

Many people go through life not realizing in every affliction, there is hope and a reason for their hardships they face every day. God does not just stand still and observe our sufferings, but He gets involved with his unseen invisible influence of love and compassion.

Larry Morton Young demonstrated a deep trust of faith and love for his Lord and Savior to show us how to walk out our faith day by day against contradicting evidence of defeat. He showed us by his example how faith is motivated by love.

When you read this book, my prayer is for your conscience mind to become more aware of what is really happening in the spirit realm of the supernatural existence in your life, while you face circumstances that try to overwhelm you and steal your joy. But, the joy of the Lord can and will be your strength, Hebrews 12:2.

God hardens us to difficulties in order to prepare us for something even greater. God wastes nothing! Isaiah 40-43.

May you too see miracles on your own journey of life as Lord reveals his love, mercy and grace to you as well as those you share this book with.

Rev. Debra Young-Waller

35

The Plan of Salvation

In 2 Peter 3:9 we read "The Lord...is not willing that any should perish, but that all should come to repentance." It is God's will the every person in His creation 'be saved' by putting their trust in Jesus, His only begotten son. Without Jesus we would all suffer the fate of eternal judgment.

John 3:16 "For God so loved the world, that He gave His only begotten son, that whosoever believes in Him should not perish, but have everlasting life."

God wants all of His children to come home to heaven and spend eternity with their loving Father.

Romans 10:9 tells us how to be saved. "If you will confess with your mouth, and if you believe in your heart that God raised Jesus from the dead, then you shall be saved."

The Lord God Almighty is waiting for you with open arms and as it says in Luke 15:10 "There is joy in the presence of the angels of God over one sinner that repents."

Debra Young Waller

Made in USA - Kendallville, IN
1188643_9781733808637
11.02.2020 0813